101 Easy Reading Games Grade 3

by Becky Daniel-White

Published by
Frank Schaffer Publications®

Author: Becky Daniel-White
Editors: Kim Bradford, Linda Triemstra

Frank Schaffer Publications ®

Send all inquiries to:
Frank Schaffer Publications
8720 Orion Place
Columbus, Ohio 43240-2111

101 Easy Reading Games—grade 3
ISBN: 0-7682-3413-1

1 2 3 4 5 6 7 8 9 MAZ 11 10 09 08 07 06

Table of Contents

0-7682-3413-1
101 Easy Reading Games

Introduction

Games are a fantastic way to teach and reinforce concepts in students of all ages. The problem with many educational games is that they are too complicated and time consuming to set up and learn. They require hours of teacher preparation and lengthy explanations to students. Something that is supposed to be fun turns out to require a lot of work.

This book addresses that problem by patterning reading games after familiar and well-loved game types, such as Bingo and Memory. By building on students' prior knowledge of game structure and rules, time can be spent actually playing the games and reinforcing target concepts.

101 Easy Reading Games is broken down into 10 major sections, according to game category. Game boards and activity pages are included in with the game instructions and game cards conveniently grouped at the back of the book. These materials and ideas will provide you and your students with hour upon hour of fun reading practice!

There are games in this book addressing all five of the key Reading First skills: phonemic awareness, decoding, fluency, vocabulary, and comprehension. You will find the games indexed by these skills on page 128.

You will find that *101 Easy Reading Games* will provide you and your students with many hours of reading fun!

0-7682-3413-1

Hangman Games

Any of the Hangman games in this section can be played two ways. The first way is like traditional hangman and hangman-type games. A word or phrase is chosen and represented on a board or paper with one blank for each letter. The player who chose the word and knows the answer fills in the blanks with letters as the other players guess them. Incorrect answers are penalized by adding on one body part at a time to the "hangman." The object of the game is for players to guess the word or phrase before the complete hangman is drawn. The person who guesses the correct answer then takes a turn choosing the word and filling in the blanks. Any object may replace the "hangman," as long as there are a designated number of parts which make up a finished object (e.g., a jack-o-lantern face at Halloween time, a cat for short *a* words, a house for settings, etc.).

The second way to play these Hangman games is Reverse Hangman. This version is played exactly like the first version, with one exception. Instead of adding parts to make a complete picture, players in Reverse Hangman begin with a complete picture and have one part erased for each incorrect letter guess.

For each game you play, decide ahead of time which way you are going to play, and what type of "hangman" figure you are going to use. Then have fun as you reinforce all sorts of reading concepts!

 ## Hangman with Decoding Pattern Words

Objective: build decoding skills with words that end in a given phoneme: -ize/-ise, -ache/-ake/-eak, or -ee/-y

Materials: one set of word cards (choose any set of cards from pages 98–100); chart paper, overhead projector, or whiteboard to write on

Getting Ready: Reproduce and cut apart the word cards. Place them in a large box or bag.

Setting: Students gather at the board.

How to Play:
1. One player is chosen to go first and draws a word.
2. The player who drew the word represents it on the board with one blank line for each letter. Before taking letter guesses, the player says, "This word ends with (the given sound)."
3. Play proceeds according to standard Hangman rules.
4. The first student to correctly guess the word is then in charge of choosing and drawing blanks for the next word. Play continues this way until you choose to stop playing.

Hangman Games

 **Hangman with Common Words**

Objective: build fluency with animal words, food words, and other common grade-appropriate words

Materials: one set of word cards (choose any set of cards from pages 101–110); chart paper, overhead projector, or whiteboard to write on

Getting Ready: Reproduce and cut apart the word cards. Place them in a large box or bag.

Setting: Students gather at the board.

How to Play:
1. One player is chosen to go first and draws a word.
2. The player who drew the word represents it on the board with one blank line for each letter. Play proceeds according to standard Hangman rules.
3. The first student to correctly guess the word is then in charge of choosing and drawing blanks for the next word. Play continues this way.

 **Hangman with Nouns and Verbs**

Objective: develop vocabulary and fluency with nouns and verbs

Materials: Noun cards (page 114), Verb cards (page 113); chart paper, overhead projector, or whiteboard to write on

Getting Ready: Reproduce and cut apart the word cards. Place them in a large box or bag.

Setting: Students gather at the board.

How to Play:
1. One player is chosen to go first, draws a word, and represents it on the board with one blank line for each letter.
2. Before accepting letter guesses, the player tells the class if the word is a noun or a verb. Play proceeds according to standard Hangman rules.

 **Hangman with Homophones**

Objective: develop vocabulary and build fluency with homophones

Materials: Homophone cards (pages 121–122); chart paper, overhead projector, or whiteboard to write on

Getting Ready: Reproduce and cut apart the word cards. Place them in a large box or bag.

Setting: Students gather at the board.

How to Play:
1. One player is chosen to go first and draws a word.
2. The player who drew the word represents it on the board with one blank line for each letter.
3. Play proceeds according to standard Hangman rules.
4. The first student to correctly guess the word must correctly define it. He then takes a turn and repeats the process with the next word.

0-7682-3413-1
101 Easy Reading Games

Hangman Games

Spelling Word Hangman

Objective: develop reading and spelling skills with current spelling words

Materials: a list of your class's spelling words; chart paper, overhead projector, or whiteboard to write on

Getting Ready: Write spelling words on pieces of paper to make word cards. Place them in a large box or bag.

Setting: Students gather at the board.

How to Play:
1. One player is chosen to go first, draws a word, and represents it on the board with one blank line for each letter.
2. Before accepting letter guesses, the player must use the word in a sentence.
3. Play proceeds according to standard Hangman rules.
4. The first student to correctly guess the word must use it correctly in another sentence. If she uses it correctly, she repeats the process with the next word.

Alternate Version: Instead of using the spelling word in a sentence, you may have players define each word, draw it, give a synonym or homophone, or act it out.

Fantasy or Reality Hangman

Objective: demonstrate ability to distinguish between fantasy and reality, and correctly identify stories as fantasy or reality

Materials: pieces of plain paper or scrap paper; chart paper, overhead projector, or whiteboard to write on

Getting Ready:
1. Pass out the small pieces of plain or scrap paper. Students think of and write one story title, and the word *fantasy* or *reality* to correctly identify the type of story it is.
3. When everyone is finished filling out their papers, collect them, fold them, and place them in a large box or bag.

Setting: Students gather at the board.

How to Play:
1. One player is chosen to go first and draws a story title out of the box.
2. The player who drew the paper represents the title on the board with one blank line for each letter in the sentence.
3. Play proceeds according to standard Hangman rules.
4. The first student to correctly guess the complete mystery title must then identify whether the story is fantasy or reality. If she correctly identifies it, she is then in charge of choosing and drawing blanks for the next fantasy or reality title. Play continues this way until you choose to stop playing.

Hangman Games

 **Story Element Hangman**

Objective: develop ability to identify basic story elements: characters, setting, problem, solution, and events

Materials: Story Element graphic organizer (see below); chart paper, overhead projector, or whiteboard to write on

Getting Ready:

1. Copy one Story Element graphic organizer for each student in your class.
2. Pass out the graphic organizers. Students choose a book or story they are familiar with and fill in the spaces with the correct information (i.e., characters, setting, problem, solution, and events).
3. When everyone is finished filling out their graphic organizers, collect all the pages, fold them, and place them in a large box or bag.

Setting: Students gather at the board.

How to Play:

1. Choose a specific element to focus on or allow each student to choose which element he is going to use.
2. One player is chosen to go first and draws a graphic organizer out of the box.
3. The player at the board writes blanks to represent his choice (e.g., — _ _ _ _ _ _ to represent *a castle* as one setting for Cinderella).
4. Before accepting letter guesses, the player must share which story element he used.
5. Play proceeds according to standard Hangman rules.
6. The first student to guess the correct answer must then identify the title of the story or book. If she identifies it correctly, she repeats the process with the next element.

Story Element Graphic Organizer

Characters	Events	Problem
Setting		Solution

Hangman Games

8 "What If" Hangman (Cause and Effect)

Objective: demonstrate ability to generate and identify corresponding causes and effects

Materials: What If cards (page 125); chart paper, overhead projector, or whiteboard to write on

Getting Ready:
1. Copy one Cause and Effect graphic organizer for each student in your class.
2. Pass out the graphic organizers. Students make up a set of corresponding causes and effects.
3. When everyone is finished filling out their graphic organizers, collect all the pages, fold them, and place them in a large box or bag.

Setting: Students gather at the board.

How to Play:
1. One player is chosen to go first and draws a graphic organizer out of the box.

2. The player represents either the cause or the effect on the board with one blank line for each letter in the sentence.
3. Before accepting letter guesses, the player must read the other sentence on the paper aloud and identify it as the cause or effect. (e.g., "The effect is 'School was canceled.' What is the cause?")
4. Play proceeds according to standard Hangman rules.
5. The first student to correctly guess the complete mystery sentence is then in charge of choosing and drawing blanks for the next word. Play continues this way until you choose to stop playing.

Alternate Version: You may also ask the student who correctly identifies the mystery sentence to give an alternate cause or effect before they are allowed to draw a new card and continue play.

Cause and Effect Graphic Organizer

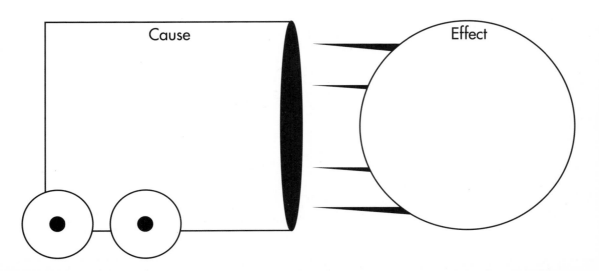

Hangman Games

9   Fact and Opinion Hangman

Objective: demonstrate ability to generate facts and opinions, and correctly identify statements as facts or opinions

Materials: Fact and Opinion graphic organizer (see below); chart paper, overhead projector, or whiteboard to write on

Getting Ready:
1. Copy one Fact and Opinion graphic organizer for each student in your class.
2. Pass out the graphic organizers. Students think of and write one fact and one opinion.
3. When everyone is finished filling out their graphic organizers, collect all the pages, fold them, and place them in a large box or bag.

Setting: Students gather at the board.

How to Play:
1. One player is chosen to go first and draws a graphic organizer out of the box.
2. The player who drew the paper represents either the fact or opinion on the board with one blank line for each letter in the sentence.
3. Play proceeds according to standard Hangman rules.
4. The first student to correctly guess the complete mystery sentence must then identify whether the statement is a fact or an opinion. If she correctly identifies it, she is then in charge of choosing and drawing blanks for the next fact or opinion. Play continues this way until you choose to stop playing.

Fact and Opinion Graphic Organizer

Fact	Opinion

Published by Frank Schaffer Publications.
Copyright protected.

0-7682-3413-1
101 Easy Reading Games

Hangman Games

 **Octopus**

Objective: reinforce animal words

Materials: Animals Word cards (pages 101–104); whiteboard to write on

Getting Ready: On the board, draw an octopus (the body and eight tentacles).

Setting: Students gather at the board.

How to Play:
1. Draw an Animal Word card. On the board, draw lines for the number of letters in the word. Provide one vowel in the

appropriate place. **Example:** *alligator* _ _ _ _ i _ _ _ _ _. Continue play according to standard Hangman rules, erasing one tentacle of the octopus for each wrong letter guess.
2. If the players can spell the animal with eight guesses (and still have the body of the octopus on the board), they win a point. If not, the teacher wins the point.
3. As you play, keep score on the board and make a list of animals.

 **Wise Flies Hangman**

Objective: reinforce words that end with -ise or -ize

Materials: -ize/-ise cards (page 98); whiteboard to write on

Getting Ready: Copy and cut apart word cards and place them in a bag. On the board, draw a simple fly. Begin with a body and add ten parts—six legs, two wings, two antenna.

Setting: Students gather at the board.

How to Play: Break into two teams and alternate turns. Play according to standard Hangman rules, but erase one fly part for each incorrect answer. Every answer that is correctly guessed before the fly is erased earns the guessing team a point. As you play, keep score on the board and make a list of rhyming words.

12 In Ten Rings

Objective: reinforce rhyming words

Materials: rhyming words list (see below); whiteboard to write on

Setting: Students gather at the board.

How to Play:
1. Think of a word that ends with *-ring*. On the board, draw ten rings and a blank for

each letter in the word. Continue play according to standard Hangman rules.
2. If the players can spell the word with ten letter guesses, they win a point. If not, the teacher wins the point. Repeat.

-*Ring* Word List: caring, sharing, daring, glaring, staring, sparing, airing, snaring, comparing, blaring, declaring, despairing, preparing, repairing

Memory

Play the games in this section like traditional memory, with cards set up facedown in a grid. Players play to see who can make the most matches.

 ## Concentrate on Endings

Objective: introduce and reinforce words with similar ending sounds

Materials: -ize/-ise cards, -ache/-ake/-eak cards, and -ee/-y cards (pages 98–100), paper cutter, rubber bands

Getting Ready: Reproduce and cut apart the word cards. Place them in a large box or bag. Divide students into teams of four.

Setting: Teams work in separate areas on the floor or outside on the grass.

How to Play:
1. Place the cards facedown in eight rows of nine cards.
2. Players take turns flipping over a pair of cards in an attempt to find words with similar ending sounds.
3. When a player makes a match, he keeps those two cards only if he correctly reads the words aloud.
4. If the two words do not rhyme, he lays the cards facedown again.
5. When all the cards have been collected, the player with the most cards is declared the winner.

 ## Animal Match

Objective: introduce and reinforce animal words

Materials: Animal Word and Picture cards (pages 101–108), cardstock, paper cutter, rubber bands

Getting Ready: For each set of three to four students, prepare a set of cards.

Setting: Three to four players sit at a table or on the floor with a deck of cards.

How to Play:
1. Shuffle the cards. (You may wish to split up one deck amongst several groups to decrease the number of animals for each game. Teams may switch decks after one game.)
2. Place the cards facedown.
3. Players take turns flipping over two cards in an attempt to make a word/picture match. When a player makes a match, he keeps those two cards if he correctly reads the animal word.
4. If a player draws two cards that are not a match, he lays them facedown again.
5. When all the matches have been made and cards collected, the player with the most cards is declared the winner.

Memory

15 Food Word Match

Objective: introduce and reinforce food words

Materials: Food cards (page 109–110), paper cutter, rubber bands

Getting Ready:
1. Reproduce a set of cards for each student.
2. Cut apart cards and secure them with a rubber band.
3. Give each student a set of cards and review words together.

Setting: Two to four players work on a flat surface, such as a floor or table.

How to Play:
Have students pair up, mix two sets of cards together, and play Memory with the combined set. They are to take turns turning over two cards to find word matches. When they find a match, they must correctly read the word to keep it. If they cannot correctly read the word, the match must be turned back over, and play passes back to the other player.

Alternate Versions:
A. Give cooperating teams three minutes to see how many matches they can make.
B. Have students glue the matches back to back to make flash cards for practicing reading and spelling the words.

16 Noun or Verb Match

Objective: introduce and reinforce nouns and verbs

Materials: Noun cards (page 114) and Verb cards (page 113), paper cutter, rubber bands

Getting Ready:
1. Reproduce a set of cards for each student.
2. Cut apart cards and secure them with a rubber band.
3. Give each student a set of cards and review words together.

Setting: Two to four players work on a flat surface, such as a floor or table.

How to Play:
Have students pair up, mix two sets of cards together, and play Memory with the combined set. They are to take turns turning over two cards to find word matches. When they find a match, they must correctly read the word and state if it is a noun or verb. If they cannot, the match must be turned back over and play passes back to the other player.

Published by Frank Schaffer Publications.
Copyright protected.

0-7682-3413-1
101 Easy Reading Games

Memory

17 Prefix Word Match

Objective: introduce and reinforce words with prefixes

Materials: Prefix Word cards (page 111), paper cutter, rubber bands

Getting Ready:
1. Reproduce a set of cards for each student.
2. Cut apart cards and secure them with a rubber band.
3. Give each student a set of cards and review words together.

Setting: Two to four players work on a flat surface, such as a floor or table.

How to Play:
Have students pair up, mix two sets of cards together, and play Memory with the combined set. They are to take turns turning over two cards to find word matches. When they find a match, they must correctly read the word and identify the prefix. If they cannot, the match must be turned back over, and play passes back to the other player.

18 Homophone Match

Objective: introduce and reinforce homophones

Materials: Homophone cards (pages 121–122), paper cutter, rubber bands

Getting Ready:
1. Reproduce a set of cards for each student.
2. Cut apart cards and secure them with a rubber band.
3. Give each pair of students a set of cards.

Setting: Two players work on a flat surface, such as a floor or table.

How to Play:
Have students play Memory. They are to take turns turning over two cards to find matches. When they find a match, they must correctly read the word to keep it. If they cannot correctly read the word, the match must be turned back over, and play passes back to the other player.

Memory

Synonym or Antonym Match

Objective: introduce and reinforce antonyms

Materials: Homophone, Synonym, Antonym cards (pages 117–120), paper cutter, rubber bands

Getting Ready:
1. Reproduce a set of cards for each student.
2. Cut apart cards and secure them with a rubber band.
3. Give each student a set of cards and review words together.

Setting: Two to four players work on a flat surface, such as a floor or table.

How to Play:
Have students pair up, using only one set of cards, and play Memory with the set. Before starting, determine if you want to play with synonyms or antonyms, and remove the extra cards. Students set up cards and take turns turning over two cards to find word matches. When they find a match, they must correctly read the words. If they cannot correctly read the words, the match must be turned back over, and play passes back to the other player.

BINGO

Play the Bingo games in this section as you do any other Bingo games. You may want to laminate Bingo boards for repeated use, and use paper or plastic chips as the Bingo markers.

 ## Color Bingo

Objective: introduce and reinforce the color words listed below

Materials: Color Word cards (below); cardstock; Bingo game card (page 17); pencils; Bingo chips

Getting Ready:
1. Reproduce a Bingo game card for each student. Reproduce one set of word cards on cardstock, then cut apart and secure with a rubber band.
2. List the color words on the board or copy the list below onto an overhead transparency.
3. As a group, practice reading the words.
4. Have students randomly write the color words on their Bingo cards, using each word at least once.
5. Pass out Bingo chips to each student.

Setting: Students sit at desks or tables with a working surface.

How to Play:
1. Shuffle word cards and stack them in a pile, facedown.
2. Draw the card off the top and read it aloud.
3. Students find the word, if they have it, and point to that square on their Bingo cards. After everyone has pointed, show and spell the word. Students pointing to the correct word may then cover it with a Bingo chip.
4. Return cards to the deck and continue until someone has Bingo—five horizontal, vertical, or diagonal squares covered.

Color Word List

apricot	aqua	cardinal	chartreuse	chestnut
chocolate	cobalt	coral	crimson	ebony
emerald	golden	indigo	ivory	jade
lavender	mauve	orange	orchid	plum
purple	sapphire	silver	turquoise	salmon

0-7682-3413-1
101 Easy Reading Games

BINGO

BINGO Game Card

B	I	N	G	O
		free		

Published by Frank Schaffer Publications.
Copyright protected.

0-7682-3413-1
101 Easy Reading Games

BINGO

21 Number Word Bingo

Objective: introduce and reinforce number words from zero to one hundred

Materials: Blank Bingo card pattern (page 17), pencils, Bingo chips

Getting Ready:
1. Across the top of blank Bingo cards, write these five combinations: 0–20, 21–40, 41–60, 61–80, and 81–100.
2. Reproduce a Bingo card for each student.

Setting: Students work at desks or tables where they can see the board.

How to Play:
1. Each student writes an appropriate number on each space of his card. **Example:** *ninety-nine* would go in the last column under 81–100.
2. One at a time, write a numeral, such as 44, on the board; don't say the number.
3. Students find the word, if they have it, and point to that square on their Bingo cards. After everyone has pointed, show and spell the word. Students pointing to the correct word may then cover it with a Bingo chip.
4. Repeat until a player has a Bingo blackout (all spaces covered).

22 Syllable Bingo

Objective: introduce and reinforce counting syllables

Materials: Bingo card pattern (page 17), dictionaries

Getting Ready:
1. Along the left margin of a Bingo card, write—one syllable, two syllables, three syllables, four syllables, and five syllables.
2. Reproduce the card for each student.
3. Pair students.

Setting: Students sit at their desks or a table with a work surface.

How to Play:
1. Players race to write an appropriate word in each space. They should indicate the syllable breaks. **Example:** Under B and in second row would be a two-syllable word that begins with b—but•ton.
2. Students may use dictionaries.
3. The first pair to cover their card with appropriate words shouts "Bingo" and is declared the winner.

Published by Frank Schaffer Publications.
Copyright protected.

0-7682-3413-1
101 Easy Reading Games

BINGO

 **Ending Sound Bingo**

Objective: introduce and reinforce words that end with the same sounds as wise, take, and royalty

Materials: -ize/-ise cards, -ache/-ake/-eak cards, and -ee/-y cards cards (pages 98–100), paper cutter, rubber bands

Getting Ready:
1. Reproduce a Bingo game card for each student. Reproduce one set of word cards on cardstock, then cut it apart and secure it with a rubber band.
2. Post the words on the board or an overhead transparency.
3. As a group, practice reading the words.
4. Have students randomly select and write words from the list onto their Bingo cards.

5. Pass out Bingo chips to each student.

Setting: Students sit at desks or tables with a working surface.

How to Play:
1. Shuffle word cards and stack them in a pile, facedown.
2. Draw the card off the top and read it aloud.
3. Students find the word, if they have it, and point to that square on their Bingo cards. After everyone has pointed, show and spell the word. Students pointing to the correct word may then cover it with a Bingo chip.
4. Return cards to the deck and continue until someone has Bingo—five horizontal, vertical, or diagonal squares covered.

 **Who? What? When? Where? Which? Bingo**

Objective: introduce and reinforce categorizing words: who, what, when, where, and which

Materials: Bingo card pattern (page 17), pencils

Getting Ready:
1. Along the left margin of the Bingo card, write Who? What? When? Where? and Which?
2. Reproduce the card for each student.

Setting: Students sit at their desks or a table with a work surface.

How to Play:
1. Players race to see who can fill each space with an appropriate word. In the first row under B will be a **who** that begins with b, such as "baby."

2. The first person to fill his card with words shouts "Bingo!"
3. Everyone stops working as he shares his list.
4. If the words are correct, he is declared the winner.
5. If not, the other players keep playing.

Alternate Version: Use the blank Bingo card on page 20 and write a five-letter word across the top before you reproduce it.
Example: **A. F. T. E. R.** Players find a who, what, when, where, and which that begins with each letter on their cards.

BINGO

Blank BINGO Game Card

		free		

Published by Frank Schaffer Publications.
Copyright protected.

0-7682-3413-1
101 Easy Reading Games

BINGO

 **Animal Bingo**

Objective: introduce and reinforce animal words

Materials: Animal Word cards (pages 101–104), blank Bingo card pattern (page 17), pencils, Bingo chips

Getting Ready:
1. Reproduce a Bingo game card for each student.
2. List the animals on the board or copy the list below onto an overhead transparency. Take turns reading them.
3. Pass out Bingo cards and Bingo chips.
4. Students choose and randomly write a word from the list in each Bingo square.

Setting: Students sit at desks or tables with a working surface.

How to Play:
1. Randomly read aloud an animal word from your list on the board or overhead.
2. Students look for the word on their Bingo sheets. If they see it, they point to it with their fingers.
3. Once everyone who thinks they have the animal word is pointing to it, read it aloud. Students who were pointing to the correct animal may cover it with a Bingo chip.
4. Continue until someone has Bingo—five horizontal, vertical, or diagonal squares covered.

alligator	alpaca	anaconda	armadillo	badger
beagle	bighorn	blackbird	bobcat	buffalo
bulldog	bullfrog	butterfly	bumblebee	centipede
cheetah	chimpanzee	cobra	coyote	crab
dinosaur	dodo	dolphin	donkey	dragonfly
eagle	electric eel	elephant	flamingo	gecko
gazelle	giraffe	gorilla	grasshopper	hamster
hedgehog	hippopotamus	hummingbird	hyena	iguana
jellyfish	kangaroo	kiwi	koala	ladybug
lizard	leopard	lobster	manatee	monkey
muskrat	mosquito	octopus	ostrich	panda
peacock	pelican	penguin	prairie dog	platypus
puffin	praying mantis	quail	rattlesnake	rhinoceros
roadrunner	salamander	scorpion	sea horse	squirrel
starfish	stingray	swine	unicorn	wallaby
walrus	whale	woodpecker	weasel	zebra

Published by Frank Schaffer Publications.

0-7682-3413-1
101 Easy Reading Games

BINGO

 **Homophone Bingo**

Objective: reinforce homophones

Materials: Homophone cards (pages 121–122); cardstock; Bingo game card (page 17); pencils; Bingo chips

Getting Ready:
1. Reproduce a Bingo game card for each student. Reproduce one set of word cards on cardstock, then cut it apart and secure it with a rubber band.
2. List the words on the board or copy pages 121 and 122 onto overhead transparencies.
3. As a group, discuss the meanings of the words and use them in sentences.
4. Have students randomly write the homophones on their Bingo cards.

5. Pass out Bingo chips to each student.

Setting: Students sit at desks or tables with a working surface.

How to Play:
1. Shuffle word cards and stack them in a pile, facedown.
2. Draw the card off the top, read it aloud, and use it in a sentence.
3. Students find the word, if they have it, and point to that square on their Bingo cards. After everyone has pointed, show and spell the word. Students pointing to the correct word may then cover it with a Bingo chip.
4. Return cards to the deck and continue until someone has Bingo—five horizontal, vertical, or diagonal squares covered.

 **Prefix Bingo**

Objective: introduce and reinforce prefixes (see list below)

Materials: blank Bingo card pattern (page 20), dictionaries, pencils

Getting Ready:
1. Along the top of the Bingo card, print the prefixes.
2. Reproduce the card for each student.
3. On the board, print the prefixes and their meanings.
4. Pair students and pass out Bingo cards.

Setting: Students sit at their desks or a table with a work surface.

How to Play:
1. Players race to fill their Bingo cards with appropriate words.
2. Players may use dictionaries to help them locate appropriate words.
3. Allow time for players to cover their cards with appropriate words.
4. The first pair to shout "Bingo" is declared the winner.

Prefixes List
re- (do again), pre- (before), un- (not), non- (not connected with), sub- (under)

BINGO

28 **Add a Suffix Bingo**

Objective: introduce and reinforce adding suffixes to root words

Materials: 23 index cards; Bingo card pattern (page 17)

Getting Ready:
1. Reproduce a Bingo card for each student.
2. Write one of the suffixes on each index card (see list below).
3. On the board, write the root word list (see list below).

Setting: Students work at desks or a table where they can see the board.

How to Play:
1. Each player writes one root word in a square on her Bingo card.
2. Draw a suffix card and call it out. Return the card to the bottom of the deck.

3. Players look at their boards and try to make a word by adding the suffix to one or more root words.
4. If a player can make a word(s) with the suffix, he writes it (them) in the appropriate square(s) on his card. **Example:** If a player has "help" and "hope," she can spell "helpful" and "hopeful." Players must include necessary spelling changes such as "angry/angrily."
6. Repeat until a player has a Bingo blackout (all spaces covered).
7. Check the spelling of the words and declare the winner!

Suffix List
-able, -age, -al, -ed, -en, -er, -est, -ful, -ing, -ish, -ist, -less, -ly, -ment, -ness, -or, -ty, -y

Root Word List
angry, bad, beauty, beg, care, close, create, false, fit, flat, force, friend, glad, help, hope, lead, like, live, plan, punish, red, sly, state, thin

29 **Noun-Forming Suffix Bingo**

Objective: introduce and reinforce noun-forming suffixes (see list below).

Materials: blank Bingo card pattern (page 20), dictionaries

Getting Ready:
1. Along the top of the Bingo card, print the noun-forming suffixes.
2. Reproduce the card for each student.
3. On the board, print the noun-forming suffixes and their meanings.
4. Pair students and pass out Bingo cards.

Setting: Students sit at their desks or a table with a work surface.

How to Play:
1. Players race to fill their Bingo cards with appropriate words.
2. Players may use dictionaries to help them locate appropriate words.
3. Allow time for players to cover their cards with appropriate words.
4. The first pair to shout "Bingo" is declared the winner.

Noun-Forming Suffixes List
-ance (state of being), -ence (quality of), -er/-or (a person who is/thing which), -ian (pertaining to), -ist (a person who)

BINGO

 **You Pick Bingo**

Objective: introduce and reinforce parts of speech: nouns, verbs, adjectives, adverbs

Materials: blank Bingo card (page 20), You Pick Word Lists (page 25)

Getting Ready:
1. Along the top of a blank Bingo card, write: person/animal, place, verb, adjective, adverb.
2. Reproduce the card and the word lists below.
3. Pass out word lists, Bingo cards, and paper chips.

Setting: Students sit at their desks or a table with a work surface.

How to Play:
1. Students are to randomly fill their Bingo cards with words from the word lists under the appropriate headings.
2. Say one of the words.
3. If a student has that word on his card, he covers it with a paper chip.
4. The first student who has five horizontal, vertical, or diagonal squares covered shouts "Bingo!"

BINGO

You Pick Word Lists

Persons/Animals Word List

aviator, beauty queen, captain, doctor, elevator operator, farmer, golfer, housekeeper, inspector, janitor, king, lawyer, mechanic, neighbor, operator, policeman, queen, repairman, senior, trapeze artist, unicyclist, violinist, waitress, x-ray technician, yodeler, zoo keeper

ant, bear, camel, dolphin, elephant, flamingo, gorilla, hamster, insect, jellyfish, kangaroo, lion, mouse, newt, octopus, penguin, queen bee, rabbit, starfish, turkey, unicorn, vole, whale, x-ray fish, yak, zebra

Places Word List

America, bottom, California, drive-in, elevator, grocery store, hospital, Iceland, Jupiter, Kansas, library, Mars, Nashville, overseas, paradise, Brooklyn, Russia, Seattle, Texas, U.S.A., vanishing point, Washington, Yellowstone Park, Mount Everest, zoo

Verbs Word List

amble, bellowed, clapped, drove, entered, fainted, glided, hid, jumped, kicked, leapt, mimicked, napped, oozed, panicked, questioned, ran, slammed, took, used, vaulted, walked, x-rayed, yodeled, zipped

Adjectives Word List

attractive, beautiful, comical, dramatic, elegant, foolish, glamorous, healthy, interesting, jumpy, kind, lovely, magnificent, nice, obvious, popular, quiet, ravishing, stunning, tiny, unique, weary, young, zealous, apricot, aqua, cardinal, chartreuse, chestnut, chocolate, cobalt, coral, crimson, ebony, emerald, golden, indigo, ivory, jade, lavender, mauve, orange, orchid, plum, purple, sapphire, silver, turquoise, salmon

Adverbs Word List

nervously, beautifully, carefully, dramatically, eagerly, fairly, gingerly, hurriedly, immediately, kindly, lovingly, masterfully, openly, perfectly, quietly, readily, speedily, timidly, vigorously, willingly, longingly, zanily

0-7682-3413-1
101 Easy Reading Games

Quiz Challenge

The Quiz Challenge games in this section may remind you of the game Jeopardy. You set up each Quiz Challenge in a similar way, with a grid of questions that are worth various point values. If you plan to play this game often, you may want to prepare a permanent Quiz Challenge board for yourself in one of the following ways.

- Construct a board out of foam board and library pockets. Write "Quiz Challenge" at the top, and attach a grid of pockets that is five across and six down. This will allow you to place the category titles at the top of each column of five questions. Label the library pockets with point values according to the pattern on page 27. You will be able to slip the cards into the pockets before each game and easily pull them out as you play.

- Purchase and set aside a cork board with push pins. Before play, write a point value on the back of each card and attach it to the board with the push pins.

- Purchase and set aside a pocket chart that has room for five columns and six rows. Make rectangular cards from cardstock that are big enough to cover the question cards, and label them with point values according to the pattern on page 27. This is a convenient way to set up your board, because cards slide easily in and out of the pockets and column headings can be seen through the clear plastic.

You may choose to select a few players for each round, break the students into teams with one spokesperson for each team, or break into small groups of four: three players and one moderator to read the cards.

Each card that has been created for this section has a category title on the top of it, as well as a point value. You may award that exact number of points, or award points in multiples of the given number (i.e., 10 or 100 for a 1 point card) for a correct answer. Keep track of points on the board or assign the job of scorekeeper to one student. He may keep track by writing the name of the person who won each question in the corresponding space on the score sheet (page 27) and adding totals at the end. Teams or individuals may compete against each other, or students may compete as a class to hit a designated target or "beat the teacher."

To add fun and excitement, create a few special bonus cards to slip in with some of the questions. Bonus ideas include "double points," "triple points," "5 extra minutes of recess," "coupon for 10 minutes of computer time," and so on.

Before play, designate a way for students to "buzz in" when they know the answer. You may have students raise hands, touch their noses, slap the table, ring a bell, use an electronic device, or make up your own method. Just be sure to be clear with students which method you are using and do your best to fairly determine who rings in first.

Card categories from different Quiz Challenge game sets may be used interchangeably as desired without affecting the game at all. Feel free to add more questions to each category as you desire, and have fun increasing reading skills as you play!

Quiz Challenge

Quiz Challenge Score Sheet

1	1	1	1	1
2	2	2	2	2
3	3	3	3	3
4	4	4	4	4
5	5	5	5	5

Published by Frank Schaffer Publications.
0-7682-3413-1
101 Easy Reading Games

Quiz Challenge

31

Homophone, Synonym, Antonym Quiz Challenge

Objective: introduce and reinforce homophone, synonym, and antonym sets

Materials: Quiz Challenge board (see introduction), Homonym, Synonym, Antonym cards (page 29), optional Quiz Challenge score sheet (page 27), cardstock, paper cutter

Getting Ready:

1. Reproduce one set of Homophone, Synonym, and Antonym cards and cut them apart. Place them in the appropriate places on your Quiz Challenge board. Create your own title cards for above the columns: Homophone, Synonym, Antonym, What Word…, and Name All 3. Any of the cards will work for all of the categories, as the **Word** is listed on top, **H** is the homophone, **S** is the synonym, and **A** is the antonym.

2. If desired, make a copy of the Quiz Challenge score sheet on paper or an overhead transparency. Write the category titles across the top.

3. Determine and communicate rules of play to the class (i.e., number of players, groups or individuals, scorekeeping, and method of "buzzing in").

Setting: Players stand or sit somewhere they can see questions and "buzz in."

How to Play:

1. The first player chooses a category and a point value (e.g., Name All 3 for 2 points).

2. Read the question.

3. Call on the first player to "buzz in."

4. The player states her answer. If correct, she is awarded the amount of points on the card. If incorrect, another player may ring in. If all students cannot answer correctly, read the correct answer and "X" out that space on the score board.

5. Continue play according to the Quiz Challenge rules until each question has been used or you are out of time.

6. Add the points to see who won.

Quiz Challenge

Homophone, Synonym, Antonym Quiz

Word: add	**Word:** ate	**Word:** bare	**Word:** bury	**Word:** beat
H: ad	**H:** eight	**H:** bear	**H:** berry	**H:** beet
S: increase	**S:** consumed	**S:** nude	**S:** entomb	**S:** weary
A: subtract	**A:** starved	**A:** dressed	**A:** uncover	**A:** energetic
Word: boy	**Word:** ceiling	**Word:** chilly	**Word:** close	**Word:** coarse
H: buoy	**H:** sealing	**H:** chili	**H:** clothes	**H:** course
S: lad	**S:** roof	**S:** cool	**S:** shut	**S:** rough
A: girl	**A:** floor	**A:** warm	**A:** open	**A:** smooth
Word: freeze	**Word:** new	**Word:** higher	**Word:** him	**Word:** whole
H: frees	**H:** gnu	**H:** hire	**H:** hymn	**H:** hole
S: chill	**S:** unused	**S:** elevated	**S:** he	**S:** all
A: boil	**A:** old	**A:** lower	**A:** her	**A:** part
Word: flee	**Word:** male	**Word:** merry	**Word:** minor	**Word:** none
H: flea	**H:** mail	**H:** marry	**H:** miner	**H:** nun
S: run	**S:** man	**S:** happy	**S:** unimportant	**S:** zero
A: stay	**A:** female	**A:** sad	**A:** major	**A:** some
Word: pale	**Word:** past	**Word:** patience	**Word:** real	**Word:** wee
H: pail	**H:** passed	**H:** patients	**H:** reel	**H:** we
S: light	**S:** before	**S:** endurance	**S:** authentic	**S:** small
A: bright	**A:** future	**A:** impatience	**A:** fake	**A:** large

Published by Frank Schaffer Publications.
Copyright protected.

0-7682-3413-1
101 Easy Reading Games

Quiz Challenge

 **Vocabulary Quiz Challenge**

Objective: expand and develop vocabulary with compound words, contractions, synonyms, antonyms, and plural words

Materials: Quiz Challenge board (see introduction), Vocabulary Quiz Challenge cards (page 31), optional Quiz Challenge score sheet (page 27), cardstock, paper cutter

Getting Ready:

1. Reproduce one set of Vocabulary Quiz Challenge cards and cut them apart. Place them in the appropriate places on your Quiz Challenge board.
2. If desired, make a copy of the Quiz Challenge score sheet on paper or an overhead transparency. Write the category titles across the top.
3. Determine and communicate rules of play to the class (i.e., number of players, groups or individuals, scorekeeping, and method of "buzzing in").

Setting: Players stand or sit somewhere they can see questions and "buzz in."

How to Play:

1. The first player chooses a category and a point value (e.g., Antonyms for 3 points).
2. Read the question.
3. Call on the first player to "buzz in."
4. The player states his answer. If correct, he is awarded the amount of points on the card. If incorrect, another player may ring in. If all students cannot answer correctly, read the correct answer and "X" out that space on the score board.
5. Continue play according to the Quiz Challenge rules until each question has been used or you are out of time.
6. Add the points to see who won.

Published by Frank Schaffer Publications.
Copyright protected.

0-7682-3413-1
101 Easy Reading Games

Quiz Challenge

Vocabulary Quiz Challenge

Compound Word Riddles	Compound Word Blanks	Antonyms	Prefixes	Suffixes
(1) Compound Word Riddles I am a cookie houses can be made of. (gingerbread)	**(1) Compound Word Blanks** The ___ goes up and down again and again. (seesaw)	**(1) Antonyms** false (true)	**(1) Prefixes** means "against" (anti-)	**(1) Suffixes** means "area ruled by" (-dom)
(2) Compound Word Riddles I am red with black spots. (ladybug)	**(2) Compound Word Blanks** The cups go in the ___. (cupboard)	**(2) Antonyms** anxious (calm)	**(2) Prefixes** means "three" (tri-)	**(2) Suffixes** means "able to" (-able)
(3) Compound Word Riddles I am black and white, and I make great music. (keyboard)	**(3) Compound Word Blanks** I think Jim just rang the ___. (doorbell)	**(3) Antonyms** artificial (real)	**(3) Prefixes** means "middle" (mid-)	**(3) Suffixes** means: "similar to" (-like)
(4) Compound Word Riddles I'm not really a cake, but I am made with cream cheese. (cheesecake)	**(4) Compound Word Blanks** The ___ was tired from herding cattle. (cowboy)	**(4) Antonyms** complex (simple)	**(4) Prefixes** means "again" (re-)	**(4) Suffixes** means "without" (-less)
(5) Compound Word Riddles I bark and I may bite, but I have no horns. (bulldog)	**(5) Compound Word Blanks** We played basketball on the hot ___. (blacktop)	**(5) Antonyms** refuse (agree)	**(5) Prefixes** means "before" (pre-)	**(5) Suffixes** means "way of being" "ness"

Published by Frank Schaffer Publications.

0-7682-3413-1
101 Easy Reading Games

Quiz Challenge

 **Homophone Quiz Challenge**

Objective: expand and develop vocabulary with homophones

Materials: Quiz Challenge board (see introduction), Homophone Quiz Challenge cards (page 33), optional Quiz Challenge score sheet (page 27), cardstock, paper cutter

Getting Ready:
1. Reproduce one set of Homophone Quiz Challenge cards and cut them apart. Place them in the appropriate places on your Quiz Challenge board.
2. If desired, make a copy of the Quiz Challenge score sheet on paper or an overhead transparency. Write the category titles across the top.
3. Determine and communicate rules of play to the class (i.e., number of players, groups or individuals, scorekeeping, and method of "buzzing in").

Setting: Players stand or sit somewhere they can see questions and "buzz in."

How to Play:
1. The first player chooses a category and a point value (e.g., Write It for 1 point).
2. Read the question.
3. Call on the first player to "buzz in."
4. The player states her answer. If correct, she is awarded the amount of points on the card. If incorrect, another player may ring in. If all students cannot answer correctly, read the correct answer and "X" out that space on the score board.
5. Continue play according to the Quiz Challenge rules until each question has been used or you are out of time.
6. Add the points to see who won.

Quiz Challenge

Homophone Quiz Challenge

Multiple Choice	Spell It	Define It	What Is This?	Write It
(1) Multiple Choice My mom's sister is my ___. a. ant b. aunt (b.)	**(1) Spell It** dents: a slight hollow (dents)	**(1) Define It** weak (not strong)	**(1) What Is This?** (bear)	**(1) Write It** *Weak* means not strong. Write <u>weak</u>. (weak)
(2) Multiple Choice Female sheep are called ___. a. ewes b. use (a.)	**(2) Spell It** real: true (real)	**(2) Define It** male (man)	**(2) What Is This?** (ant)	**(2) Write It** *Their* means it belongs to them. Write <u>their</u>. (their)
(3) Multiple Choice I started a letter "___ Bill," a. Dear b. deer (a.)	**(3) Spell It** wail: to cry (wail)	**(3) Define It** dense (thick)	**(3) What Is This?** (yak)	**(3) Write It** When you get together with people, you *meet* them. Write <u>meet</u>. (meet)
(4) Multiple Choice A rabbit is a ___. a. hair b. hare (b.)	**(4) Spell It** pale: not dark (pale)	**(4) Define It** heart (body organ)	**(4) What Is This?** (whale)	**(4) Write It** The library books are *due*. Write <u>due</u>. (due)
(5) Multiple Choice At night my mom listens to the ___. a. gnus b. news (b.)	**(5) Spell It** our: belongs to us (our)	**(5) Define It** pail (bucket)	**(5) What Is This?** (hair)	**(5) Write It** A *cell* is a small room. Write <u>cell</u>. (cell)

0-7682-3413-1
101 Easy Reading Games

Quiz Challenge

 **Comprehension Quiz Challenge**

Objective: expand and develop comprehension skills

Materials: Quiz Challenge board (see introduction), Comprehension Quiz Challenge cards (page 35), optional Quiz Challenge score sheet (page 27), cardstock, paper cutter

Getting Ready:

1. Reproduce one set of Comprehension Quiz Challenge cards and cut them apart. Place them in the appropriate places on your Quiz Challenge board.
2. If desired, make a copy of the Quiz Challenge score sheet on paper or an overhead transparency. Write the category titles across the top.
3. Determine and communicate rules of play to the class (i.e., number of players, groups or individuals, scorekeeping, and method of "buzzing in").

Setting: Players stand or sit somewhere they can see questions and "buzz in."

How to Play:

1. The first player chooses a category and a point value (e.g., Cause & Effect for 4 points).
2. Read the question.
3. Call on the first player to "buzz in."
4. The player states his answer. If correct, he is awarded the amount of points on the card. If incorrect, another player may ring in. If all students cannot answer correctly, read the correct answer and "X" out that space on the score board.
5. Continue play according to the Quiz Challenge rules until each question has been used or you are out of time.
6. Add the points to see who won.

Quiz Challenge

Comprehension Quiz Challenge

Classify: Which Doesn't Belong	Classify: Name This Group	Riddles (Conclusions)	Prediction	Cause & Effect
(1) Classify: Which Doesn't Belong? stapler, marker, pen, mug (mug)	**(1) Classify: Name This Group** knife, scissors, razor (things that cut)	**(1) Riddles (Conclusions)** I am a huge cat with a mane. I also have sharp teeth. What am I? (lion)	**(1) Prediction** What might happen on your next vacation? (answers vary)	**(1) Cause & Effect** It snowed all night long. What is the effect? (snow-covered ground, snow day, etc.)
(2) Classify: Which Doesn't Belong? spoon, coin, book, can (book)	**(2) Classify: Name This Group** carpet, tile, wood (types of floors)	**(2) Riddles (Conclusions)** I look like a horse with black and white stripes. What am I? (zebra)	**(2) Prediction** What might happen next spring? (answers vary)	**(2) Cause & Effect** Bill has a cavity in one tooth. What caused it? (not brushing, sugar, etc.)
(3) Classify: Which Doesn't Belong? chocolate, bread, cookies, cake (bread)	**(3) Classify: Name This Group** fork, spoon, knife (utensils)	**(3) Riddles (Conclusions)** I am big and brown. I sleep all winter. What am I? (bear)	**(3) Prediction** Kim forgot her homework. What might happen next? (answers vary)	**(3) Cause & Effect** Mia studied her spelling words. What will be the effect? (good grade on test)
(4) Classify: Which Doesn't Belong? keyboard, phone, monitor, mouse (phone)	**(4) Classify: Name This Group** whale, person, lion (mammals)	**(4) Riddles (Conclusions)** I have humps on my back and I live in the desert. (camel)	**(4) Prediction** Your mom runs out of gas. What might happen next? (answers vary)	**(4) Cause & Effect** Steve is nice to his friends. What will be the effect? (friends will be nice back to him, etc.)
(5) Classify: Which Doesn't Belong? seesaw, slide, pool, monkey bars (pool)	**(5) Classify: Name This Group** Saturn, Mars, Venus (planets)	**(5) Riddles (Conclusions)** I am a huge animal. My big nose is called a trunk. What am I? (elephant)	**(5) Prediction** You stay up too late. What might happen next? (answers vary)	**(5) Cause & Effect** What could have caused Amy's broken arm? (a fall, an accident, etc.)

Published by Frank Schaffer Publications.

0-7682-3413-1

101 Easy Reading Games

Quiz Challenge

35 Story Elements Quiz Challenge

Objective: demonstrate comprehension of a specified story by identifying story elements

Materials: Quiz Challenge board (see introduction), Story Elements Quiz Challenge cards (page 37), optional Quiz Challenge score sheet (page 27), cardstock, paper cutter

Getting Ready:

1. Reproduce one set of Story Elements Quiz Challenge cards and cut them apart. Place them in the appropriate places on your Quiz Challenge board.
2. If desired, make a copy of the Quiz Challenge score sheet on paper or an overhead transparency. Write the category titles across the top.
3. Determine and communicate rules of play to the class (i.e., number of players, groups or individuals, scorekeeping, and method of "buzzing in").

Setting: Players stand or sit somewhere they can see questions and "buzz in."

How to Play:

1. Use this game to review a book or story everyone has read. Answers are not given on the cards, so the moderator must determine what the correct answers are for each question.
2. The first player chooses a category and a point value (e.g., Character for 5 points).
3. Read the question.
4. Call on the first player to "buzz in."
5. The player states his answer. If correct, he is awarded the amount of points on the card. If incorrect, another player may ring in. If all students cannot answer correctly, read the correct answer and "X" out that space on the score board.
6. Continue play according to the Quiz Challenge rules until each question has been used or you are out of time.
7. Add the points to see who won.

Quiz Challenge

Story Elements Quiz Challenge

Character	Setting	Problem	Solution	Events
(1) Character Who is the main character in this story?	**(1) Setting** Where does this story take place?	**(1) Problem** What is the main problem in this story?	**(1) Solution** How is the main problem in this story solved?	**(1) Events** What happened in the beginning of this story?
(2) Character Name two other characters in this story.	**(2) Setting** When does this story take place?	**(2) Problem** Was there one problem in this story or more than one?	**(2) Solution** Was the main problem in this story solved on the first try?	**(2) Events** What happened in the middle of this story?
(3) Character Give two details describing the main character in this story.	**(3) Setting** In this story, was there one setting or more than one?	**(3) Problem** Name one character that had a problem in this story. Describe the problem.	**(3) Solution** How many times did the characters in this story try to solve the problem?	**(3) Events** What happened at the end of this story?
(4) Character Give four details describing one of the other characters in this story.	**(4) Setting** Give three details that describe the setting of this story.	**(4) Problem** Could the problem in this story really happen? Why or why not?	**(4) Solution** Could the main problem really be solved the way it is in this story? Why or why not?	**(4) Events** Could the events in this story really happen? Why or why not?
(5) Character Name a character from another story that is similar to a character in this story.	**(5) Setting** Name a story with a similar setting to the one in this story.	**(5) Problem** Name a story with a similar problem to the one in this story.	**(5) Solution** Name a story with a similar solution to the one in this story.	**(5) Events** Name a story with a similar sequence of events to the events in this story.

Published by Frank Schaffer Publications.
Copyright protected.

0-7682-3413-1
101 Easy Reading Games

Quiz Challenge

36 Fairy Tale Quiz Challenge

Objective: demonstrate comprehension of story elements for a variety of fairy tales

Materials: Quiz Challenge board (see introduction), Fairy Tale Quiz Challenge cards (page 124), optional Quiz Challenge score sheet (page 27), cardstock, paper cutter

Getting Ready:

1. Reproduce one set of Fairy Tale Quiz Challenge cards and cut them apart. Place them in the appropriate places on your Quiz Challenge board.
2. If desired, make a copy of the Quiz Challenge score sheet on paper or an overhead transparency. Write the category titles across the top.
3. Determine and communicate rules of play to the class (i.e., number of players, groups or individuals, scorekeeping, and method of "buzzing in").

Setting: Players stand or sit somewhere they can see questions and "buzz in."

How to Play:

1. The first player chooses a category and a point value (e.g., Lesson Learned for 4 points).
2. Read the question.
3. Call on the first player to "buzz in."
4. The player states his answer. If correct, he is awarded the amount of points on the card. If incorrect, another player may ring in. If all students cannot answer correctly, read the correct answer and "X" out that space on the score board.
5. Continue play according to the Quiz Challenge rules until each question has been used or you are out of time.
6. Add the points to see who won.

Alternate Version: Combination Quiz Challenge

Play according to regular Quiz Challenge rules. Combine different sets of Quiz Challenge cards or write your own. Use this format as a fun way to review materials you have covered or to preview new material.

Quiz Challenge

Fairy Tale Quiz Challenge

Characters	Setting	Name the Fairy Tale with This Problem	Name the Fairy Tale with This Solution	Lesson Learned
(1) Characters She was tiny, could fly, and was bright as a light. (Tinkerbell)	**(1) Setting** Peter Pan lived here. (Never-Never-Land)	**(1) Problem** Two kids were lost and hungry. ("Hansel and Gretel")	**(1) Solution** He became a real boy. ("Pinocchio")	**(1) Lesson** Beauty is in the eye of the beholder. ("Beauty and the Beast")
(2) Characters They built their own houses. (The 3 Little Pigs)	**(2) Setting** The Little Red Hen lived here. (farm)	**(2) Problem** His nose grew when he lied. ("Pinocchio")	**(2) Solution** She called him by name. ("Rumpelstiltskin")	**(2) Lesson** Never trust a hungry fox. ("The Gingerbread Man")
(3) Characters He was eaten by a fox. (The Gingerbread Man)	**(3) Setting** Jack climbed a beanstalk to this place. (sky/giant's house)	**(3) Problem** He underestimated his opponent. ("The Tortoise and the Hare")	**(3) Solution** They found a girl sleeping in a bed. ("Goldilocks and the 3 Bears")	**(3) Lesson** You can't fool everyone. ("The Emperor's New Clothes")
(4) Characters She wore a scarlet head cover. (Little Red Riding Hood)	**(4) Setting** Red Riding Hood met the wolf here. (Grandma's house/ woods)	**(4) Problem** He didn't think the lady would ever guess his name. ("Rumpelstiltskin")	**(4) Solution** A little boy shouted out and everyone saw the truth. ("The Emperor's New Clothes")	**(4) Lesson** A thing worth doing is worth doing well. ("The Three Little Pigs")
(5) Characters He thought the world was ending. (Chicken Little)	**(5) Setting** Hansel and Gretel got in trouble here. (The witch's house)	**(5) Problem** He played mean practical jokes. ("The Boy Who Cried Wolf")	**(5) Solution** The world didn't end after all. ("Chicken Little")	**(5) Lesson** Be kind, even to those who mistreat you. ("Cinderella")

Published by Frank Schaffer Publications. Copyright protected.

0-7682-3413-1
 101 Easy Reading Games

Quick Draw

The purpose of Quick Draw is to develop and demonstrate vocabulary and comprehension skills. Students will deepen their understanding of words, concepts, and story elements as they are challenged to show what they visualize when reading. These games also are a great way to address different learning styles and allow students with visual and artistic skills to shine!

The Quick Draw games in this section all follow a simple format—one player sketches a designated word while others shout out guesses. This may be played as a whole class, as teams, or with partners.

In the whole-class version, one artist at a time draws a word as class members earn points to hit a target number.

The team version still involves the whole class in group play, but teams take turns drawing. The team whose turn it is has a time limit for each word. If they are unable to guess correctly in the time allowed, the other team has a chance to "steal" the point by correctly guessing the word. Play alternates between the two teams. Teams earn points to compete with each other and the team with the most points at the end is the winner.

For partner play, students pair up. Each pair has one set of cards to draw from. Players take turns drawing and guessing.

However you choose to play, Quick Draw is a great way to practice vocabulary and comprehension!

 Draw and Spell Plurals

Objective: introduce and reinforce spelling the plurals of food words

Materials: Food cards (pages 109–110), scissors, paper bag

Getting Ready:
1. Reproduce the food cards.
2. Cut apart cards.
3. Fold each card once. Place them in a paper bag.
4. Divide students into four teams.

Setting: Teams gather at the board.

How to Play:
1. Players take turns drawing a picture card from the bag and, on the board, drawing more than one of the food listed on the card.
2. Teammates call out answers. When someone guesses correctly, the player drawing writes the plural word on the board. If he spells it correctly, he wins a point for his team.
3. As you play, keep score on the board and make two lists of words—singular words and plural words.

Quick Draw

38 Combining Forces

Objective: introduce and reinforce twenty-four verbs and twenty-four nouns

Materials: Verb cards (page 113), Nouns cards (page 114), scissors, two paper bags, whiteboard (or overhead, chalkboard, or chart paper)

Getting Ready:
1. Reproduce the word cards.
2. Cut apart cards and fold each one.
3. Place the verbs in one bag and the nouns in another.
4. Divide students into two teams.

Setting: Teams gather at the board.

How to Play:
1. The first player draws a word from each bag. He then draws a picture on the board that represents the noun (subject) doing the verb (action).
2. All players may shout out their answer.
3. The first player to correctly name the noun and verb wins a point for his team and gets to be It next.
4. The first team to get 10 points is declared the winner.

Quick Draw

39   Numeric Prefixes

Objective: introduce and reinforce numeric prefixes (see list below).

Materials: Prefixes word cards (page 112), scissors, paper bags, whiteboard (or overhead, chalkboard, or chart paper)

Getting Ready:

1. Reproduce the word cards.
2. Cut apart cards and fold each one.
3. Place the Numeric Prefix cards in a paper bag.
4. On the board, list the prefixes and their meanings.
5. Divide students into four teams.

Setting: Teams gather at the board.

How to Play:

1. Players take turns drawing a word from the bag.
2. Player uses fingers (fist for one-half) to indicate the prefix and then draws a picture on the board to convey the word.
3. All players may shout out their answer.
4. The first player to correctly name the word wins a point for his team and gets to be It next.
5. The first team to get six points is declared the winner.
6. As you play, keep score on the board and make a word list.

Numeric Prefixes Word List

semi- (half), mono- (one), bi- (two), tri- (three), quad- (four), penta- (five), hex- (six), sept- (seven), oct- (eight), dec- (ten), multi- (many)

Quick Draw

 **Draw a Dodo**

Objective: introduce and reinforce animal words

Materials: Animal Word cards (pages 101–104), whiteboard (or overhead, chalkboard, or chart paper), scissors, paper bag, stopwatch

Getting Ready:
1. Reproduce the cards.
2. Cut apart cards and fold each one.
3. Place the cards in a paper bag.
4. Divide students into three or four teams.

Setting: Teams gather at the board.

How to Play:
1. The first player draws a word from the bag, and then draws a picture of the animal on the board.
2. Team members shout out their guesses. If a team member guesses correctly in less than two minutes, that team wins a point.
3. If that team cannot guess correctly in two minutes, another team gets a chance to guess.
4. As you play, keep score on the board and make an animal word list.

 **Draw Your Own Conclusion**

Objective: introduce and reinforce ability to draw conclusions

Materials: Situation cards (page 126)

Getting Ready: Reproduce the cards (one sheet per student). Don't cut apart.

Setting: Students gather at the board.

How to Play:
1. Pass out the sheets.
2. Students are to choose one, think of an ending, and draw a picture of it.
3. Other players guess the situation.

Board Games

The board games in this section follow the general pattern of board games involving a game board with a start and an end, game markers for each player, and cards with questions on them. You may choose to use the game board provided in this section, make up your own, or use game boards you have from other games. The cards and instructions will work with any of these type of simple game boards and any game markers. To make the game board on pages 42–43, match the two sides at the dotted lines and tape together.

 ## Zoo Hike

Objective: introduce and reinforce animal words

Materials: game board patterns (pages 46–47), Animal Word cards (pages 101–104), sturdy cardstock, scissors, glue stick, markers, game markers (paper chip with student's initials, name, etc.), paper cutter, rubber bands

Getting Ready:
1. For each set of three to four players, reproduce a game board and set of cards on sturdy cardstock.
2. Trim and glue the game board to the inside of a file folder. Decorate with markers, stickers, etc.
3. Cut apart animal picture cards and secure each deck with a rubber band.

Setting: Two to four players sit at a table around the game board.

How to Play:
1. Shuffle cards and place facedown on game board.
2. Players place their markers in the "start" space.
3. The first player turns over the top card and reads aloud the name of the animal. If he is correct, he moves ahead the number of letters in the word. If he is incorrect, he doesn't advance on the board.
4. Place the animal card on the bottom of the deck.
5. Repeat with the next player.
6. The player who reaches Finish first is declared the winner.

Published by Frank Schaffer Publications.
Copyright protected.

0-7682-3413-1
101 Easy Reading Games

Board Games

43   Hungry Plurals

Objective: introduce and reinforce the plural forms of food words

Materials: game board patterns (pages 46–47), Food Pictures cards (pages 109–110), sturdy cardstock, scissors, glue stick, markers, paper cutter, rubber bands, game markers (paper chip with student's initials, name, etc.)

Getting Ready:
1. For each set of three to four players, reproduce a game board and set of cards on sturdy cardstock.
2. Trim and glue game board to inside of a file folder. Decorate with markers, stickers, etc.
3. Cut apart Food Pictures cards and secure each deck with a rubber band.

Setting: Two to four players sit at a table around the game board.

How to Play:
1. Shuffle cards and place facedown on game board.
2. Players place their markers in the "start" space.
3. The first player turns over the top card, reads the word, and states the plural form of the food. If he is correct, he moves ahead the number of letters in the word. If he is incorrect, he doesn't advance on the board.
4. Place the card facedown on the bottom of the deck.
5. Repeat with the next player.
6. The player who reaches Finish first is declared the winner.

Published by Frank Schaffer Publications.
Copyright protected.

0-7682-3413-1
101 Easy Reading Games

Board Games

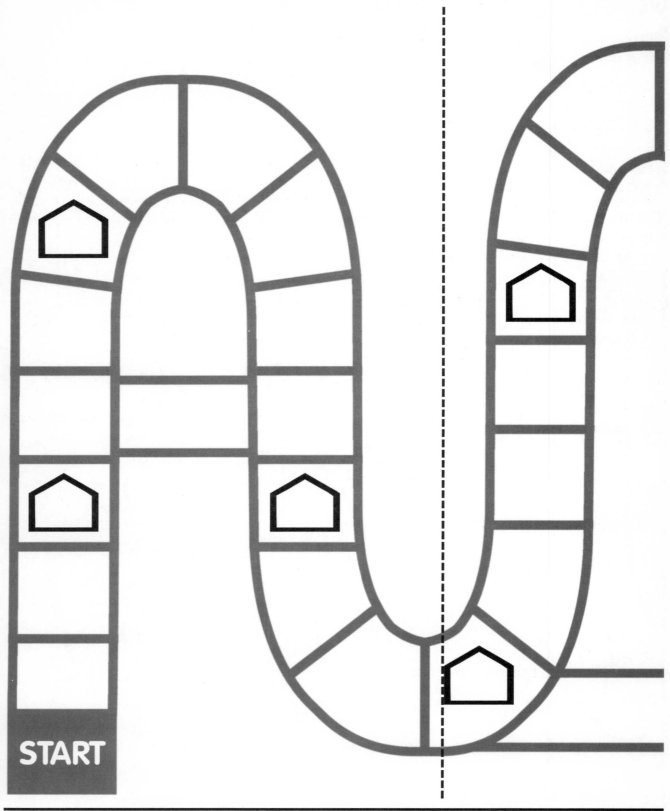

START

0-7682-3413-1
101 Easy Reading Games

Board Games

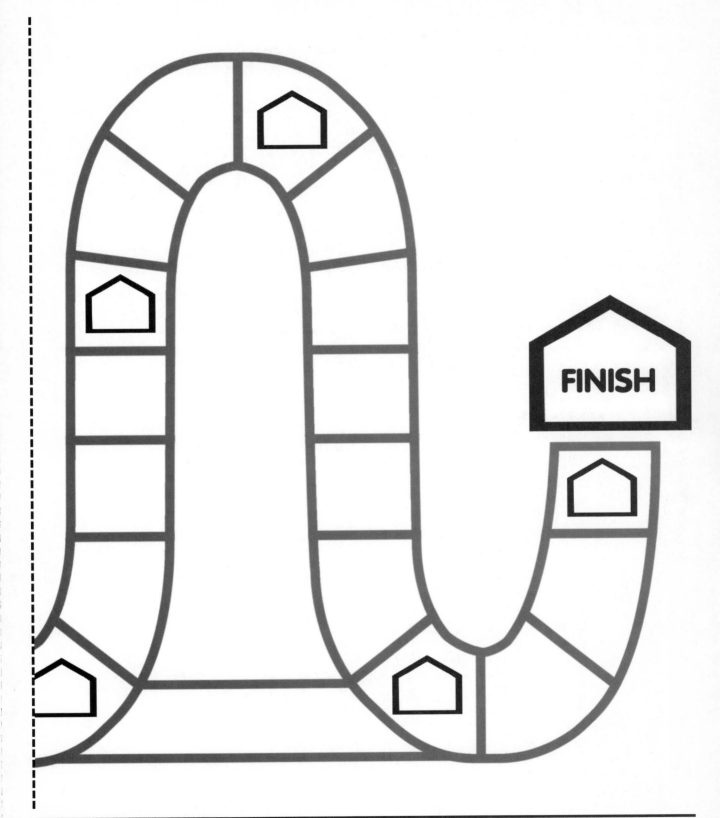

FINISH

0-7682-3413-1
101 Easy Reading Games

Board Games

Prefix Race

Objective: introduce and reinforce words with prefixes

Materials: game board pattern (pages 46–47), Prefix Word cards and Numeric Prefix cards (pages 111–112), sturdy cardstock, paper cutter, rubber bands, game markers (paper chip with student's initials, name, etc.)

Getting Ready:
1. For each set of three to four players, reproduce a game board and word cards on sturdy cardstock.
2. Trim and glue game board to inside of a file folder. Decorate with markers, stickers, etc.
3. Cut apart cards and secure each deck with a rubber band.

Setting: Two to four players sit at a table around the game board.

How to Play:
1. Shuffle cards and place facedown on game board.
2. Players place their markers in the "start" space.
3. The first player draws a card and reads it aloud.
4. If he is correct, he keeps the card and moves ahead the number of letters in the word.
5. If he is incorrect, he places the card facedown on the bottom of the deck and doesn't advance his marker.
6. The player who reaches Finish first is declared the winner.

Published by Frank Schaffer Publications.
Copyright protected.

0-7682-3413-1
101 Easy Reading Games

Board Games

 **Prefix-Suffix Race**

Objective: introduce and reinforce twenty root words with prefixes and suffixes

Materials: game board pattern (pages 46–47), Root Word cards (page 116) sturdy cardstock, scissors, glue stick, markers, game markers (paper chip with student's initials, name, etc.) paper cutter, rubber bands, dice

Getting Ready:

1. In the empty spaces on the game board, write a prefix or a suffix (see lists below).
2. For each set of three to four players, reproduce a game board and two sets of word cards on sturdy cardstock.
3. Trim and glue game board to inside of a file folder.
4. Cut apart cards and secure each deck (two of each kind) with a rubber band.

Setting: Two to four players sit at a table around the game board.

How to Play:

1. Shuffle cards and place them facedown.
2. Players place their markers in the "start" space.
3. The first player rolls the dice and advances marker the number indicated by the dice. Then he draws a card. If the player can use the prefix or suffix his piece is resting on with the root word on his card, he gets to keep the card. If the player cannot make a word, he puts the card facedown on the bottom of the deck.
4. Repeat with the next player.
5. When all cards have been collected, count to see who has the most.

Prefixes List

un-, non-, in-, dis-, re-, semi-, mini-, micro-, inter-, super-, trans-, ex-, extra-, peri-, pre-, anti-, fore-, post-, macro-, over-

Suffixes List

-ance, -ence, -or, -er, -ist, -ize, -ate, -fy, -ness, -ify, -able, -ible, -ing, -ic, -ical, -ish, -ive, -ly, -ed, -en

Published by Frank Schaffer Publications.
Copyright protected.

0-7682-3413-1
101 Easy Reading Games

Board Games

 **Rhyming Race**

Objective: introduce and reinforce rhyming words

Materials: whiteboard (or overhead, chalkboard, or chart paper), game board pattern (pages 46–47), -ize/-ise cards, -ache/-ake/-eak cards, and -ee/-y cards (pages 98–100), sturdy cardstock, scissors, glue stick, markers, game markers (paper chip with student's initials, name, etc.), paper cutter, rubber bands

Getting Ready:

1. For each set of three to four players, reproduce a game board and set of word cards on sturdy cardstock.
2. Trim and glue the game board to inside of a file folder.
3. Cut apart word cards and secure each deck with a rubber band.

Setting: Two to four players sit at a table around the game board.

How to Play:

1. Shuffle cards and place facedown on game board.
2. Players place their markers in the "start" space.
3. The first player draws a card. If he can read it, he moves ahead the number of letters in the word and keeps the card.
4. If he cannot read the word, he places the card facedown on the bottom of the deck and doesn't advance his marker.
5. The player who reaches Finish first is declared the winner.

Board Games

47   Fairy Tale Spin

Objective: introduce and reinforce elements of story structure: character, setting, problem, outcome, and lesson learned

Materials: whiteboard (or overhead, chalkboard, or chart paper), game board pattern (pages 46–47), Fairy Tale cards (page 124), sturdy cardstock, scissors, glue stick, markers, paper cutter, game markers (paper chip with student's initials, name, etc.), dice

Getting Ready:
1. On each blank space of the game board, randomly print each of the five story parts several times: character, setting, problem, outcome, and lesson.
2. For each set of three to four players, reproduce a game board and two sets of cards on sturdy cardstock.
3. Cut apart the forty-eight cards (two of each kind) and secure each deck with a rubber band.

Setting: Two to four players sit at a table around the game board.

How to Play:
1. Shuffle cards and place them facedown.
2. Players place their markers in the "start" space.
3. The first player rolls a die and advances his marker that many spaces. Then he draws a card.
4. If the player can give the appropriate information for the card he drew and the space he landed on, he keeps the card.
5. If the player cannot give the information, he returns the card, facedown, to the bottom of the deck.
6. Repeat with the next player.
7. When all of the cards have been collected, count to see who has the most.

Board Games

48 Definition, Please

Objective: introduce and reinforce words with prefixes of location and numbers (see lists below).

Materials: game board pattern (pages 46–47), Prefix cards (page 111–112), sturdy cardstock, scissors, glue stick, markers, game markers (paper chip with student's initials, name, etc.), paper cutter, rubber bands

Getting Ready:
1. For each set of three to four players, reproduce a game board and set of word cards on sturdy cardstock.
2. Trim and glue the game board to inside of a file folder.
3. Cut apart word cards and secure each deck with a rubber band.

Setting: Two to four players sit at a table around the game board.

How to Play:
1. Shuffle the cards and place facedown on the game board.
2. Players place their markers in the "start" space.
3. The first player draws a card, and without looking at the board or the answer key, he gives a definition of the word, including the number meaning of the prefix.
   Example: octagon (eight-sided figure).
4. If he is correct, he moves ahead the number of letters in the word. If he is incorrect, he doesn't advance his marker.
5. Place the card facedown on the bottom of the deck.
6. The player who reaches Finish first is declared the winner.

Locations Word List
inter- (between, among)
super- (over)
trans- (across)
ex- (out)
extra- (beyond)
sub- (under)
infra- (below)
peri- (around)

Numbers Word List
semi- (half)
mono- (one)
bi- (two)
tri- (three)
quad- (four)
penta- (five)
hex- (six)
sept- (seven)
oct- (eight)
dec- (ten)
multi- (many)

Card Games

This section contains games designed to play like such timeless classics as Solitaire, War, and Rummy. You may choose to play other card games, such as Old Maid, as well. The cards lend themselves well to many more games than there is room to list!

 Animal Rummy

Objective: introduce and reinforce classifying animal words

Materials: Animal Word cards (pages 101–104), sturdy cardstock, paper cutter, rubber bands

Getting Ready:
1. For every four players, reproduce a set of cards.
2. Cut apart the cards and secure each deck with a rubber band.
3. List the four categories on the board: same initial letter, can fly, can swim, same number of legs.

Setting: Four players sit at a table or on the floor.

How to Play:
1. Shuffle the cards.
2. Deal seven cards to each player.
3. Players look for four cards that fit in one of the categories and lay them faceup in front of them. Each time a player lays down cards, on his next turn, he draws enough cards to be holding seven.
4. Players take turns drawing the top card from deck (or the last card discarded faceup by the previous player) and discarding a card.
5. After all the cards have been turned over, the player with the most matches is declared the winner.

 Homophone Rummy

Objective: introduce and reinforce homophone pairs

Materials: Homophone cards (pages 121–122), sturdy cardstock, paper cutter, rubber bands

Getting Ready:
1. For each pair of players, reproduce cards and cut apart.
2. Secure each deck of cards with a rubber band.

Setting: Pairs sit at a table or on the floor.

How to Play:
1. Shuffle the cards.
2. Deal seven cards to each player.
3. Players look for homophone matches and lay them down faceup in front of them.
4. Players take turns drawing the top card from deck (or the last card discarded faceup by previous player) and discarding a card.
5. After all the cards have been turned over, shuffle the discard pile and continue playing.
6. The first player to make three matches is declared the winner.

Published by Frank Schaffer Publications.
Copyright protected.

0-7682-3413-1
101 Easy Reading Games

Card Games

 **Homophone, Synonym, Antonym Rummy**

Objective: introduce and reinforce homophones, antonyms, and synonyms

Materials: Homophone, Synonym, Antonym cards (pages 117–120), sturdy cardstock, paper cutter, rubber bands

Getting Ready:
1. For every two to four players, reproduce a set of cards.
2. Cut apart the cards and secure each deck with a rubber band. (Do not cut page 117. Players use this to check answers.)

Setting: Three to four players sit at a table or on the floor.

How to Play:
1. Shuffle the cards.
2. Deal seven cards to each player.
3. The object is to get a four-way match (a homophone pair plus a synonym and an antonym for one of the homophones). **Example:** add, ad, increase, subtract.
4. Players take turns drawing the top card from deck (or the last card discarded face-up by previous player) and discarding a card.
5. After all the cards have been turned over, shuffle the discard pile and continue playing.
6. The first player to make a four-way match is the winner of that round.

 **Animal Solitaire**

Objective: introduce and reinforce animal words

Materials: Animal Word cards (pages 101–104), paper cutter, rubber bands

Getting Ready:
1. Reproduce a set of Animal Word cards for each student.
2. Cut apart cards and secure each deck with a rubber band.

Setting: Players work on the floor or outside in the grass.

How to Play:
1. Players mix up their cards and place the deck facedown.
2. One at a time, players turn over a card.
3. The object is to make a square of three words across and three rows down that is in ABC order (reading left to right).
4. After a card has been placed, it cannot be moved.

Sample Game

If player draws *beagle* next, he wouldn't be able to put it in ABC order and so he wouldn't win that round. If he draws *monkey,* it would fit in ABC order, and he would win.

badger	coyote	crab
dodo	eagle	gecko
kiwi	lizard	

Published by Frank Schaffer Publications.
Copyright protected.

0-7682-3413-1
101 Easy Reading Games

Card Games

 **Rhyming War**

Objective: introduce and reinforce forty-eight rhyming words

Materials: -ize/-ise cards and -ache/-ake/-eak cards (pages 98–99), sturdy cardstock, paper cutter, rubber bands

Getting Ready: Each pair of students needs a set of cards.

Setting: Two players sit facing each other.

How to Play:
1. Shuffle the cards and deal out all of them to the two players.
2. One player chooses "rhymes" and the other player is then "doesn't rhyme."
3. At the same time, both players turn over their top card.

4. If the cards rhyme, the player who chose "rhymes" reads the words aloud. If he can read them, he keeps both cards. If he cannot read them, this opponent gets a chance to read them. If the opponent reads them, he keeps the cards. If neither can read them, those cards go into a discard pile.
5. If the cards don't rhyme, the player who chose "doesn't rhyme" gets to try to read the words first.
6. Continue until all the cards have been turned over once.
7. Count to see who collected the most cards.

Alternate Version: Use the -ee/-y cards (page 100) plus either the -ize/-ise cards or -ache/-ake/-eak cards to play the game again.

 **War of Plurals**

Objective: introduce and reinforce the plural forms of forty food words

Materials: Food cards (pages 109–110), sturdy cardstock, paper cutter, rubber bands

Getting Ready:
1. Reproduce a set of cards for each pair of students.
2. Cut apart cards and secure each deck with a rubber band.

Setting: Two players sit facing each other and use only one deck of cards.

How to Play:
1. Shuffle the deck of cards and place facedown.
2. The first player turns over the top card.
3. If the player can spell the plural of the food word, he keeps the card.
4. If he cannot spell it, the other player gets a chance to spell it and keep the card.
5. If neither player can spell the word, the card goes into the discard pile.
6. Continue until all the food cards have been turned over.
7. Count to see who collected the most cards.

Silly Stories

The Silly Stories in this section are played the same way as other fill-in-the-blank activities such as Mad Libs. Review word categories with students before playing, and, if you wish, make word lists for each of the categories used: relatives, person/people, names, things, colors, days and months, animals, body parts, food, actions, numbers, nouns, verbs, and adjectives.

 **Silly Story Fables**

Objective: introduce and reinforce categories of words—nouns, verbs, adjectives

Materials: "The Hungry Wolf and the Lost Lamb" (page 57), pencil

Getting Ready: Reproduce the fable five times.

Setting: Students gather around the board.

How to Play:
1. Let a volunteer fill in the blanks with words as you ask for them.

2. Repeat two more times, filling in the blanks of the same fable with input from different players.
3. Read aloud all versions of the fable.
4. Compare the versions:
   • Which one was the funniest?
   • Which words made the fable interesting?
5. Read the original fable (see below).
6. Take turns predicting the lesson Aesop offered in his fable "The Hungry Wolf and Lost Lamb."

The Hungry Wolf and the Lost Lamb

One day a hungry wolf spotted a lost lamb. The wolf resolved not to be beastly but to find justification for eating the lamb. The wolf said, "Lamb, last year you insulted me."

""Thaaaaaat's not true," bleated the lamb. "Last year I was not yet born."

Then said the wolf, "You are eating grass in my pasture. Do you deny that?"

"Yeeeees, I do deny that," replied the lamb, "because I have not yet eaten grass."

The wolf said angrily, "You drink out of my stream."

"Nooooo," exclaimed the lamb, "I never drink water. My mother's milk is both food and drink to me."

The wolf grew weary of the debate and grabbed the lamb and ate him up, saying, "Well! I can't remain hungry, even though you refute my every word."

Published by Frank Schaffer Publications.
Copyright protected.

0-7682-3413-1
101 Easy Reading Games

Name _____ Date _____

Silly Story #1
The Hungry Wolf and the Lost Lamb

One day a _____, _____, spotted a
             (adjective)   (animal #1)

_____ _____. The _____,
(adjective)   (animal #2)   (adjective)

_____, resolved not to be _____ but to find
(animal #1)   (adjective)

justification for _____ _____ _____.
                        (verb)   (adjective)   (animal #2)

The _____ said, "_____, _____
       (animal #1)   (animal #2)   (time)

you _____ed me."
         (verb)

"Thaaaaaat's not true," _____ the _____.
                              (verb)   (animal #1)

"_____ I was not yet born." Then said the _____,
    (time)   (animal #1)

"Well, you are _____ing grass in my _____. Do you deny that?"
                  (verb)   (place)

"Yeeeees, I do deny that," replied the _____, "because I have
                                          (animal #2)

not yet _____ grass." The _____ said angrily, "You
            (verb)   (animal #1)

_____ out of my stream." "Nooooo," exclaimed the _____
    (verb)   (animal #2)

"I never _____ _____. My mother's milk is both food and
            (verb)   (food)

and drink to me." _____ grew weary of the debate and
                       (animal #1)

_____ the lamb and _____ him up, saying, "Well!
     (verb)   (verb)

I can't remain _____, even though you _____ my every
                     (verb)   (verb)

word."

Silly Stories

 **Mad Fables in Triplet**

Objective: introduce and reinforce categories—nouns, verbs, adjectives

Materials: original fables (page 59) and silly fables (pages 60–62)

Getting Ready: Reproduce enough silly stories so each team of three will have one of each.

Setting: Teams of three meet in a place where they can write. Each person receives a different fable.

How to Play:
1. One person reads and fills in the blanks as directed by a partner.
2. When the blanks are filled, the scribe reads the new version of the fable to the partners.
3. Repeat with all three members of the group.
4. Meet in a large group, and have students read the fables to each other.
5. Compare and contrast the fables.
6. Read the originals and compare with the new versions.

Silly Stories

Three Aesop's Fables

The Two Dogs

A man had two dogs. One dog was trained to help him hunt. The other dog was trained to watch the house. When the man and the hunting dog returned home after a good day's work, the man always gave the house dog a large share of the meat.

The hunting dog didn't think it was fair. He said, "It is very hard to do all the work, while you, who do not help, get as much meat as I."

The other dog replied, "Do not blame me. It is the fault of the man who has not trained me to work. Now I am weak and must depend upon you, or I will starve."

The Lion and the Boar

One summer day, when the hot sun made all the animals thirsty, a lion and a boar came to a small well. Both being stubborn, soon the lion and the boar were fighting about which should be allowed to drink first. After battling for hours, both were nearly dead. Suddenly they stopped to catch their breath. It was then that they saw some vultures flying overhead. At once the lion and the boar made up their minds not to fight.

The Donkey's Shadow

A man rented a donkey to carry him to a distant place. The donkey's owner went along to bring his donkey home.

The day was intensely hot. After a few hours, the traveler stopped to rest and sought shelter under the donkey.

When the owner of the donkey saw the traveler resting comfortably in the shadow of his donkey, he said, "Get up and let me rest there. You rented my donkey only—not its shadow."

The traveler asserted that he, with the rent of the donkey, also should receive the benefit of its shadow.

The quarrel proceeded from words to blows. And while the two fought, the donkey galloped off toward home, where his cool barn awaited him.

Published by Frank Schaffer Publications.

0-7682-3413-1
101 Easy Reading Games

Silly Story #1

Two Animals

_____ had two _____s.
(name of student)   (animal #1)

One _____ was _____ to _____
(animal #1)   (verb)   (verb)

_____ hunt. The other _____ was
(name of student)   (animal)

_____ to _____ the _____
(verb)   (verb)   (noun)

When _____ and the hunting _____
(name of student)   (animal)

returned home after a _____ day's work, _____
(adjective)   (student's name)

always gave the _____ _____ a
(verb)   (animal)

_____ share of the _____.
(size/amount)   (food #1)

The hunting _____ didn't think it was fair. He said,
(animal)

"It is very _____ to do all the work, while you,
(adjective)

who do not _____, get as much _____ as I."
(verb)   (food #1)

The other _____ replied, "Do not _____ me. It is the fault
(animal #1)   (verb)

of _____ who has not _____ me to hunt.
(student's name)   (verb)

Now I am weak and must depend upon you or I will _____."
(verb)

60

Name _____   Date _____

Silly Story #2

Bitter Battle

One _____ day, when the _____ sun
      (season)   (adjective)

made all the animals _____, a _____ and a _____
                 (verb)   (animal #1)   (animal #2)

came to a _____ well. Both being _____,
      (adjective of size)   (adjective)

soon the _____ and _____ were _____ing about
      (animal #1)   (animal #2)   (verb)

which should be allowed to _____ first.
                   (verb)

After _____ for hours, both were nearly dead.
      (verb)

Suddenly they _____ to _____ their breath.
       (verb)   (verb)

It was then that they _____ some _____ _____ overhead.
           (verb)   (animal #3)   (verb)

At once the _____ and the _____ made up their minds
      (animal #1)   (animal #2)

not to _____.
      (verb)

                101 Easy Reading Games

Name _____ Date _____

Silly Story #3

The Shadow

_____ rented a _____ to carry him (her)
　(student #1)　　　　　　　　　　　　　(animal)

to _____. The _____'s owner, _____
　(distant place)　　　　　(animal)　　　　　　　　(student #2)

went along, to bring the _____ home.
　　　　　　　　　　　　　(animal)

　　The day was _____ hot. After a _____ hours,
　　　　　　　　　　(adjective)　　　　　　　　(number)

_____ stopped to rest and sought shelter under the
　(student #1)

_____.
　(animal)

　　When _____, owner of the _____ saw
　　　　　　(student #2)　　　　　　　　　　(animal)

_____ resting _____ly in the shadow of
　(student #1)　　　　　　　　(adjective)

his/her _____, he/she said, "Get up and let me rest there.
　　　　　(animal)

You rented my _____ only—not its shadow."

_____ asserted that he/she, with the rent of
　(student #1)

the _____, also should receive the benefit of its shadow.
　　(animal)

The quarrel proceeded from words to blows. And while

_____ and _____ fought, the
　(student #1)　　　　　　(student #2)

_____ _____ed off toward home, where
　(animal)　　　　　　(verb)

its _____ _____ awaited.
　(adjective)　　　　　(kind of building)

101 Easy Reading Games

Silly Stories

57 Fable Dramas

Objective: reinforce categories of words—nouns, verbs, adjectives

Materials: fables game sheets (pages 64–66)

Getting Ready: Reproduce game sheets so that each group of three will have a copy of each fable.

Setting: Teams of three meet where they can write and move around.

How to Play:
1. Each member of the group picks a fable and fills in the blanks.
2. Team members take turns reading the new versions to each other.
3. The team picks one story to dramatize.
4. Allow plenty of time for rehearsal.
5. In a large group, share the new versions of the fables.

Alternate Version: Read the original version of each of the fables.

The Father and Two Daughters

A man had two daughters. One daughter was a gardener. The other was a tile maker. One day the man went to the gardener and asked how things were.

She said, "All things are prospering. I have only one wish. In order that the plants may be well watered, I wish for rain."

Not long after, the man went to the tile maker and asked how she fared. She said, "I want for nothing. I have only one wish. So that my bricks will dry, I need the sun to be hot and bright."

The man thought: One daughter needs rain. The other needs dry weather. With which of them am I to join my wish?

Three Travelers

Three travelers climbed to the top of a tall cliff overlooking the sea. In the distance they saw what they thought was a large ship. They sat down and waited so they could see the ship enter the harbor.

As the object came nearer to harbor, they realized that it couldn't be a ship, but only a small boat. After nearly an hour, when it reached the beach, the three saw that it was neither a ship nor a boat—only a stick. One said to his companions, "We have wasted our day waiting. There is nothing here to see but a stick of wood."

The Battle

A great city was at war. Its citizens were called together to decide the best means of protecting it from the enemy. A bricklayer earnestly recommended bricks as the best material for an effective resistance. A carpenter, with equal zeal, proposed timber as the preferable method of defense. Upon which a hunter yelled, "Sirs, I differ with you both. There is no material for resistance equal to a covering of hides—nothing so good as leather."

The men fought on into the night. Meanwhile their enemies captured the unprotected city.

Published by Frank Schaffer Publications.
Copyright protected.

0-7682-3413-1
101 Easy Reading Games

Name _____ Date _____

Silly Story #4

The Father (Mother)

_____ had two daughters, _____ and _____.
(group member #1)   (member #2)   (member #3)

_____ was a _____. _____
(member #2)   (occupation #1)   (member #3)

was a _____. One day _____
(occupation #2)   (member #1)

went to _____ and asked how things were.
(member #2)

_____ said, "All things are prospering. I have only one
(member #2)

wish. In order that the _____ may be _____, I
(product of occupation #1)   (verb #1)

wish for _____."
(certain kind of weather)

Not long after, _____ went to _____
(member #1)   (member #3)

and asked how she fared. _____ said, "I want for nothing.
(member #3)

I have only one wish. So that my _____ will _____,
(product of occupation #2) (verb)

I need the _____ to be _____ and _____."
(opposite weather)   (describe opposite weather)

_____ thought: _____ needs _____.
(member #1)   (member #2)   (product #1)

_____ needs _____. With which am I to join my wish?
(member #3) (opposite weather)

Published by Frank Schaffer Publications.
Copyright protected.

0-7682-3413-1
101 Easy Reading Games

Name _____ Date _____

Silly Story #5

Three Travelers

_____, _____, and _____
(group member #1)   (group member #2)   (group member #3)

climbed to the top of a _____ overlooking _____.
(place #1).   (place #2)

In the distance _____, _____, and _____
(member #1)   (member #2)   (member #3)

saw what they thought was a _____ _____.
(adjective #1)   (object #1)

They sat down and waited so they could see the _____
(adjective #1)

_____ enter the _____. However, as the
(object #1)   (place #3)

object came nearer to _____, they realized that it
(place #3)

couldn't be a _____ _____, but only a
(adjective #1)   (object #1)

_____ _____. After nearly an hour, when
(adjective #2)   (object #2)

it reached them, _____, _____, and _____
(member #1)   (member #2)   (member #3)

saw that it was neither a _____ _____
(adjective #1)   (object #1)

nor_____ _____—only a _____
(adjective #2)   (object #2)   (adjective #3)

_____. _____ said to his companions,
(object #3)   (member #1)

"We have wasted our day waiting. There is
nothing here to see but a _____ _____."
(adjective #3)   (object #3)

0-7682-3413-1
101 Easy Reading Games

Silly Story #6

The War

A _____ city was at war. Its citizens
         (adjective)

were called together to decide the best means of protecting it from the

enemy. _____, a _____ earnestly
       (group member #1)   (occupation #1)

recommended _____ as the best material for an
            (product of occupation #1)

_____ resistance. _____, a
       (adjective)   (group member #2)

_____, with equal zeal, proposed _____
    (occupation   (product of occupation #2)

as the preferable method of defense. Upon which _____,
                                                    (member #3)

a _____ yelled, "Sirs, I differ with you both.
   (occupation #3)

There is no material for resistance equal to a _____
                                                  (product of occupation #3)

—nothing so good as _____."
                    (product of occupation #3)

_____, _____, and _____ fought on into the night.
(member #1)   (member #2)   (member #3)

Meanwhile their enemies captured the _____ city.

Anytime Brain Builders

58 Clueless

Objective: introduce and reinforce rhyming words

Materials: Clueless cards (page 97), paper bag, whiteboard (or overhead, chalkboard, or chart paper), stopwatch

Getting Ready:
1. Reproduce cards.
2. Cut apart cards and fold once.
3. Place the cards in a paper bag.
4. Explain that the clue contains a word that rhymes with the answer. Demonstrate how to emphasize the rhyming word when giving the clue. **Example:** sing to me in the *shade*—three syllables *(serenade)*
5. Divide students into two teams.

Setting: Teams gather at the board.

How to Play:
1. The first player draws a card from the bag and reads it aloud.
2. The team has one minute to take turns guessing the rhyming word.
3. If someone on the team names the word, the team gets as many points as there are letters in the word.
4. If they cannot name the word, the other team gets to guess.
5. As you play, keep score on the board and make a rhyming word list.

59 Concentrate on Syllables

Objective: introduce and reinforce dividing words into syllables

Materials: -ize/-ise cards, -ache/-ake/-eak cards, and -ee/-y cards (pages 98–100), paper cutter, rubber bands, answer key

Getting Ready:
1. Reproduce a set of word cards.
2. Divide students into teams of four.

Setting: Teams gather at the board.

How to Play:
1. Members of each team stand at the board.
2. Read one of the rhyming word cards.
3. Students write the word, including syllable marks. Correct answers win each of those players a point for his team.
4. As you play, keep score on the board and make a word list including syllable marks.

Anytime Brain Builders

 **Beat the Clock**

Objective: introduce and reinforce words with matching homophones, synonyms, and antonyms

Materials: Homophone, Synonym, Antonym cards (page 117), sturdy stock, paper cutter, rubber bands, stopwatch

Getting Ready:
1. Reproduce the cards for each pair in your group.
2. Cut apart cards and secure each deck with a rubber band.
3. Give each pair a deck of cards.

Setting: Pairs of students sit at a table facing each other.

How to Play:
1. Shuffle deck of Homophone, Synonym, and Antonym cards.
2. As the teacher times three minutes, one player in each pair chooses a card and quizzes the partner on the antonym, synonym, or homophone of the given word.
3. The player names a synonym, antonym, or homophone as quickly as he can, and the correct cards go in his stack.
4. If the player doesn't know a word, he can call "pass," and the card goes back into the quiz stack.
5. At the end of three minutes, time is called.
6. Count how many cards the player collected.
7. Repeat with the other partner reading the cards.
8. At the end of three more minutes, count how many cards the player read.
9. Help pairs total their scores to see which

 Race to Make a Sentence

Objective: introduce and reinforce nouns and verbs

Materials: Noun cards and Verb cards (pages 113–114), sturdy cardstock, paper cutter, rubber bands

Getting Ready:
1. Reproduce the cards for each pair in your group.
2. Cut apart cards and secure each deck with a rubber band.
3. Have students pick a partner.

Setting: Pairs sit facing each other.

How to Play:
1. Sort the cards into two stacks—nouns and verbs—and shuffle both decks.
2. The first player turns over the top card on each stack.
3. He then must give a five-word sentence including the noun and verb. **Example:** The trapeze artist will juggle.
4. If he can make a sentence, he keeps the cards. If he cannot, the other player gets the cards.
5. After twelve rounds of play, count to see which player has the most cards.

Anytime Brain Builders

 **Caging the Animals**

Objective: sort animal words into a variety of categories

Materials: Animal Word cards (pages 101–104), scissors

Getting Ready:
1. Reproduce the word cards for each member of the class.
2. Cut apart cards and secure each deck with a rubber band.
3. Pair students.

Setting: Pairs gather in the classroom or outside on the grass.

How to Play: Ask questions. Players race to sort cards.
1. How many animals that begin with "g" have four legs? (4—gecko, giraffe, gorilla, gazelle)
2. How many are animals beginning with "d" are extinct? (2—dinosaur, dodo)

3. How many animals beginning with "p" can fly? (1—pelican)
4. How many animals beginning with "a" have four legs? (2—alpaca, armadillo)
5. How many of the eighty animals can fly? (16)
6. How many animals that begin with "a" live in water? (1—alligator)
7. How many of the eighty animals are compound words? (17—blackbird, bobcat, bulldog, bullfrog, butterfly, bumblebee, dragonfly, grasshopper, hedgehog, hummingbird, jellyfish, ladybug, rattlesnake, roadrunner, starfish, stingray, woodpecker)
8. How many animals that begin with "b" can fly? (3—blackbird, butterfly, bumblebee)
9. How many animals that begin with "e" cannot fly? (2—electric eel, elephant)
10. How many animals beginning with "k" can fly? (1—kiwi)

63 What's Wrong Here?

Objective: develop fluency skills by fixing common punctuation and spelling errors

Materials: sentence list (see below), whiteboard (or overhead, chalkboard, or chart paper), answer key

Setting: Four teams gather at the board.

How to Play: A member of each team stands at the board. Write a sentence without punctuation, including misspellings. The first player who rewrites the sentence correctly wins a point for his team. As you play, keep score on the board.

Sentence List
1. max are you going to the party
2. we ate pie ice cream and cookies
3. if you dont go we can not go
4. sue you mispelled one word
5. each one finished their work
6. does that windmill wind in the wind
7. george will stay but regan cant
8. juan you collect snakes snails and slugs
9. oh dear I lost the money
10. its true a snail carries its home on its back

Published by Frank Schaffer Publications.
Copyright protected.

0-7682-3413-1
101 Easy Reading Games

Anytime Brain Builders

64 **Ode to the Pointers**

Objective: introduce and reinforce twenty words that rhyme with *ode* (see list below)

Materials: whiteboard (or overhead, chalkboard, or chart paper), two pointers

Getting Ready:

1. On the board, draw the *rhymes with "ode"* squares (see picture below).
2. Pair students.

Setting: Players gather at the board.

How to Play:

1. One pair at a time holds the pointers.
2. Say a word that rhymes with *ode*.
3. Each member of the pair points to a section on one of the squares.
4. If the pair correctly spells the word, they get the same number of points as letters in the word.

5. If the team cannot point out the letters to spell the word, the pointers are handed to the next pair, who tries to point them out.
6. Repeat until every team has had several turns to spell a word.
7. As you play, keep score on the board and make a list of rhyming words.

Rhyming Words List

load	road
overload	rode
payload	code
unload	decode
a la mode	erode
abode	explode
commode	strode
corrode	toad

l	t	r	c
ar	er	unl	str
dec	corr	expl	comm
overl	ster	payl	ab

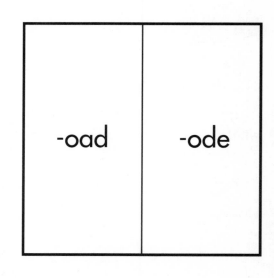

-oad | -ode

Anytime Brain Builders

65 Shout About *Out*

Objective: introduce and reinforce twenty-four words that rhyme with *out* (see list below in the Challenges)

Materials: whiteboard (or overhead, chalkboard, or chart paper), Challenges

Getting Ready:
1. Explain that every answer will be a word that rhymes with *out.*
2. Divide students into three or four teams.

Setting: A player from each team stands at the board.

How to Play:
1. Read the clue. Repeat as necessary.
2. The first player who prints the correct answer wins a point for her team.
3. Give the next clue to other members of each team.
4. As you play, keep score on the board and make a rhyming word list.

Challenges
1. It begins with "ab" and rhymes with *out.* (about)
2. When a city has no lights, it is called a _____. (blackout)
3. He who does scouting activities is a _____. (Boy Scout)
4. She who has influence over others has _____. (clout)
5. A dedicated man is sometimes said to be _____. (devout)
6. To worry and not trust someone is to _____. (doubt)
7. He who doesn't complete schooling is called a _____. (dropout)
8. When there is no rain, it is called a _____. (drought)
9. Baseball players sit here. (dugout)
10. She can build a campfire and tie knots. (Girl Scout)
11. A place to be with friends is a _____. (hangout)
12. To have a scowl on your face is to _____. (pout)
13. Going about something indirectly is the _____ way. (roundabout)
14. A cabbage dish is called _____. (sauerkraut)
15. To call out loudly is to _____. (shout)
16. Anteaters have a big one. (snout)
17. Most teapots have one. (spout)
18. Gardens do this first. (sprout)
19. Chinese food taken home to eat is called _____. (takeout)
20. If it's cooked all the way through it is done _____. (throughout)
21. Some like to fish for this. (trout)
22. People have to do this to get a part in a play. (try out)
23. Where the water comes out. (waterspout)
24. Not to have is to go _____. (without)

Anytime Brain Builders

 **66** **Achy Breaky Heart**

Objective: introduce and reinforce words that rhyme with *ache* (see list below)

Materials: whiteboard (or overhead, chalkboard, or chart paper), -ache/-ake/-eak cards (page 99), paper cutter, rubber bands

Getting Ready:
1. Reproduce a set of cards for each pair of students.
2. Cut apart cards and secure each deck with a rubber band.
3. Have students pick a partner.

Setting: Pairs sit at desks or tables with a working surface.

How to Play:
1. One at a time, give a challenge.
2. Pairs race to sort their cards and answer with a show of fingers. (They must cooperate because it might take fingers on all four of their hands to answer a challenge.)
3. The first pair with the correct number of fingers shown reads aloud those cards. If they are correct, the pair wins the number of points as cards in that group.
4. As you play, keep score on the board.

Word List

awake, backache, beefcake, bellyache, coffeecake, cornflake, cupcake, daybreak, earthquake, forsake, fruitcake, handshake, heartache, johnnycake, mistake, namesake, opaque, outbreak, pancake, rattlesnake, shortcake, snowflake, sweepstake, undertake

Challenges
1. How many can you eat? (9—beefcake, coffeecake, cornflake, cupcake, fruitcake, johnnycake, pancake, shortcake, snowflake)
2. How many are compound words? (20—backache, beefcake, bellyache, coffeecake, cornflake, cupcake, daybreak, earthquake, fruitcake, handshake, heartache, johnnycake, namesake, outbreak, pancake, rattlesnake, shortcake, snowflake, sweepstake, undertake)
3. How many have a long "e" ? (3—beefcake, coffeecake, sweepstake)
4. How many are painful? (3—backache, bellyache, heartache)
5. How many are animals? (1—rattlesnake)
6. How many have a short "u"? (2—cupcake, undertake)
7. How many are things done with your hands? (1—handshake)
8. How many have a long "o"? (2—opaque, snowflake)
9. How many have a "ch" that sounds like "k"? (3—backache, bellyache, heartache)
10. How many are breakfast foods? (answers may vary; 4—coffeecake, cornflake, johnnycake, pancake)
11. How many are desserts? (4—coffeecake, cupcake, fruitcake, shortcake)
12. How many have two syllables? (19—awake, backache, beefcake, cornflake, cupcake, daybreak, earthquake, forsake, fruitcake, handshake, heartache, mistake, namesake, opaque, outbreak, pancake, shortcake, snowflake, sweepstake)

Published by Frank Schaffer Publications.
Copyright protected.

0-7682-3413-1
101 Easy Reading Games

Anytime Brain Builders

 **Rhyming Zoo**

Objective: introduce and reinforce rhyming animal words

Materials: Rhyming Zoo game sheet (page 74), pencils, paper, dictionaries, stopwatch

Getting Ready:
1. Reproduce game sheet for each pair of students.
2. Explain that all of the answers will be an animal. Two-word animals and compound words are acceptable.
3. Have students pick a partner.

Setting: Pairs sit at separate tables or areas on the floor.

How to Play:
1. Allow 20 minutes for teams to look in dictionary and list all the animals they can find that rhyme with each animal on the list.
2. After 20 minutes, count to see which pair listed the most animals.

Possible Answers

cat—bat, bobcat, muskrat, rat, gnat, wombat

bee—donkey, flea, honeybee, chimpanzee, chickadee, collie, kiwi, manatee, monkey, wallaby

dog—bulldog, hog, frog, hedgehog

crow—buffalo, doe, mosquito, swallow, dodo, armadillo, flamingo

walrus—rhinoceros, porpoise

dingo—hippo, rhino

goat—coyote (Western pronunciation)

tiger—salamander, caterpillar, badger, lobster, grasshopper, roadrunner

zebra—piranha, cheetah, Chihuahua, llama, panda, iguana, gorilla, boa, anaconda, alpaca, koala, cobra, impala, hyena

centipede—millipede

eagle—beagle

0-7682-3413-1
101 Easy Reading Games

Name _____ Date _____

Rhyming Zoo Game Sheet

cat

_____
_____
_____
_____
_____
_____

bee

_____
_____
_____
_____
_____
_____
_____
_____

dog

_____
_____
_____
_____

crow

_____
_____
_____
_____
_____

walrus

_____
_____
_____

dingo

_____
_____

goat

_____
_____
_____

tiger

_____
_____
_____
_____
_____
_____

zebra

_____
_____
_____
_____
_____
_____
_____
_____
_____
_____
_____
_____
_____

centipede

_____

eagle

_____

Total Score

_____

Published by Frank Schaffer Publications.
Copyright protected.

0-7682-3413-1
101 Easy Reading Games

Anytime Brain Builders

68 Sorting Rhymes

Objective: introduce and reinforce rhyming words

Materials: -ize/-ise cards, -ache/-ake/-eak cards, and -ee/-y cards (pages 98–100), paper cutter, rubber bands

Getting Ready
1. Reproduce a set of word cards for each student.
2. Cut apart cards and secure each deck with a rubber band.

Setting: Players work at a desk or table with a work surface.

How to Play:
1. Mix up cards.
2. On the word "go," players race to sort cards into three piles according to their ending sounds.
3. The first person to finish is declared the winner.

Alternate Version: Sort according to nouns, verbs, adjectives, or adverbs.

69 Zoo Keepers

Objective: introduce and reinforce animal words

Materials: Animal Word cards (pages 101–104), cardstock, pencils, scissors, dictionaries, markers

Getting Ready: On cardstock, reproduce the word cards for each member of the class.

Setting: Pairs meet with pencils and paper, in the classroom or outside on the grass.

How to Play:
1. Students cut apart cards.
2. On the back of each card, they draw a picture of the animal. They may use dictionaries to help find illustrations.
3. Pair students.
4. Partners take turns flashing the card to each other, first to identify the animal name, then for the spelling of words.

Published by Frank Schaffer Publications.
Copyright protected.

0-7682-3413-1
101 Easy Reading Games

Anytime Brain Builders

70   I'm Thinking of Something

Objective: reinforce phonemic awareness, decoding, vocabulary, and comprehension skills

Materials: none

Getting Ready: none

Setting: anywhere

How to Play: This game is another versatile and easy way to reinforce reading skills any time and anyplace.

1. Begin by thinking of a word or concept that you can use as your mystery word or phrase.
2. Say, "I'm thinking of…" and go on to describe something about the word (see examples below).
3. Students take turns guessing.

4. The first student to guess it correctly takes the next turn. Continue this way for as long as time allows.

Examples:

- Phonemic Awareness: "a word with 3 syllables," "an animal that rhymes with *peel*"
- Decoding: "a word that starts with a 'tr' blend," "a word with a long 'a' sound"
- Vocabulary: "a homophone that means *calm* or *a part*," "a compound word you can wear in the water"
- Comprehension: "the problem in *The Gingerbread Man*," "something that causes a broken window"
- Combined Skills: "a synonym for *job* that has a short 'a' sound"

71   20 Questions

Objective: reinforce vocabulary and comprehension skills

Materials: none

Getting Ready: none

Setting: anywhere

How to Play: This game is another versatile and easy way to reinforce reading skills any time and anyplace.

1. Begin by thinking of a word or concept that you can use as your mystery word or phrase.

2. Say, "I'm thinking of…" and give one clue about the word (e.g., a homophone, a compound word, a character, and so on).
3. Students take turns asking *yes* or *no* questions about the word. The players are allowed unlimited *yes* answers, but only 20 *no* answers.
4. The first student to guess the word correctly takes the next turn. If nobody guesses correctly with twenty or less "no" answers, reveal the answer and begin again with a new word. Continue this way for as long as time allows.

Anytime Brain Builders

72 Say It Again

Objective: practice phonemic awareness skills

Materials: none

Getting Ready: none

Setting: anywhere

How to Play:

1. Choose any word. You may wish to play with mixed word and skill types or focus on a specific type of phoneme (e.g., initial consonants/blends, suffixes, or syllables—see examples below). Tell players, "Say (the word)."
2. Players say the word.
3. Tell the players, "Say it again, but don't say (one phoneme/part of the word)."
4. Repeat for as many words as you want to work on, playing for points if you wish.

Examples:

- <u>Compound Words:</u> "Say *mailbox*. Say it again but don't say *box*." (mail)
- <u>Initial Consonants/Blends:</u> "Say *black*. Say it again but don't say *ack*." (bl)
- <u>Final Consonants/Blends:</u> "Say *beast*. Say it again but don't say *st*." (bea
- <u>Prefixes/Suffixes:</u> "Say *redo*. Say it again but don't say *re*." (do)
- <u>Syllables:</u> "Say *popsicle*. Say it again but don't say *sic*." (pop-le)
- <u>Vowel Sounds/Blends:</u> "Say *tree*. Say it again but don't say *ee*.

Anytime Brain Builders

 **Prefix or Suffix Word Categories**

Objective: reinforce words with prefixes and suffixes

Materials: whiteboard, list of prefixes and suffixes you want to work on, stopwatch

Getting Ready: Divide the students into teams of four to six members.

Setting: Teams gather at the board.

How to Play:
1. The first player from each team stands at the board.
2. Name a prefix or suffix.
3. Players have sixty seconds to list as many words with that prefix or suffix as they can.
4. Each correct word a player lists is a point for his team.
5. As you play, keep score on the board.

 **Other Categories**

Objective: demonstrate ability to generate words with given sounds or syllables, details for a given main idea, story elements, synonyms, vocabulary that fits a given profile, causes and effects, or facts and opinions

Materials: whiteboard, list of reading skills or words you want to work on, stopwatch

Getting Ready: Divide the students into teams of four to six members.

Setting: Teams gather at the board.

How to Play:
1. The first player from each team stands at the board.
2. Name a category.
3. Players have sixty seconds to list as many words with that initial blend as they can.
4. Each correct word a player lists is a point for his team.
5. As you play, keep score on the board.

Examples

Words with given sounds or syllable: -ing words, long "a" words, short "o" words, words from the "-ale" word family, animals beginning with "r," words with two syllables

Details for a given main idea: feelings, calendar words, healthy foods, toys, birds, things you might find in a city, community helpers, things you do when you're happy

Story elements: animal character names, fantasy settings, problems involving school

Vocabulary: compound words, words with "ball" in them, homophone sets, antonym pairs, actions words (verbs), describing words (adjectives), plural nouns, words that could describe rotting food, science vocabulary words

Published by Frank Schaffer Publications.
Copyright protected.

0-7682-3413-1
101 Easy Reading Games

Anytime Brain Builders

75 Sorting It Out

Objective: introduce and reinforce classifying animals

Materials: Animal Word cards (pages 101–104), paper cutter, rubber bands

Getting Ready:
1. Reproduce a set of word cards for each student.
2. Cut apart cards and secure each deck with a rubber band.

Setting: Students sit at desks or tables with a work surface.

How to Play:
1. One at a time, give a challenge.
2. Players race to sort their cards and indicate answers with a show of fingers.
3. The first player to show the correct number of fingers gets to answer.
4. If his answers are correct, he wins a point for each card in that set.
5. As you play, keep score on the board and make a list of words, including syllable marks.

Challenges
1. How many animal words that begin with an "a" have four syllables? (3—al•li•ga•tor, an•a•con•da, ar•ma•dil•lo)
2. How many one-syllable animals are there? (4—crab, quail, swine, whale)
3. How many three-syllable animal names begin with "h"? (2—hum•ming•bird, hy•e•na)
4. How many two-syllable animal names begin with "b"? (6—bad•ger, bea•gle, black•bird, bob•cat, bull•dog, bull•frog)
5. How many animal names are five-syllable words? (1—hip•po•pot•a•mus)
6. How many words have a long "o" in the last syllable? (5—ar•ma•dil•lo, buf•fa•lo, do•do, geck•o, mos•qui•to)
7. How many names that begin with "s" have more than two syllables? (2—sal•a•man•der, scor•pi•on)
8. How many animal names are compound words? (17—black•bird, bob•cat, bull•dog, bull•frog, but•ter•fly, grass•hopper, hedge•hog, humming•bird, jelly•fish, la•dy•bug, musk•rat, rat•tle•snake, road•run•ner, sting•ray, star•fish, pea•cock, wood•pecker)
9. How many animal names that begin with "d" have two syllables? (3—do•do, dol•phin, don•key)
10. How many animal names have four syllables? (6—al•li•ga•tor, an•a•con•da, ar•ma•dil•lo, cat•er•pil•lar, rhi•noc•er•os, sal•a•man•der)
11. How many two-syllable animal names begin with "g"? (3—geck•o, gir•affe, ga•zelle)
12. How many syllables are in the only word beginning with "u"? (3—u•ni•corn)
13. What is the sum of the syllables for the three animal names beginning with "k"? (eight—kan•ga•roo, ki•wi, ko•a•la)
14. How many animal words have a long "e" in the last syllable? (5—cen•ti•pede, chim•pan•zee, coy•o•te, don•key, mon•key)
15. How many words rhyme with "us"? (4—hip•po•pot•a•mus, plat•y•pus, rhi•noc•er•os, wal•rus)

0-7682-3413-1
101 Easy Reading Games

Anytime Brain Builders

76 Noun-Forming Suffixes

Objective: introduce and reinforce noun-forming suffixes (see list below)

Materials: Noun-Forming Suffixes cards (page 115), rubber bands, whiteboard (or overhead, chalkboard, or chart paper)

Getting Ready:
1. Prepare cards for each student.
2. On the board, write a list of suffixes and the ways they change meaning.

Setting: Students play at desks or a table with a work surface.

How to Play: Give the word clues, and players race to find the word and receive a point. As you play, keep score (the first five people to find each card) and make a word list on the board.

Suffixes List

-ance (state of), -ence (quality of), -er/-or (a person who/a thing which), -ist/-yst (a person who), -ian (pertaining to), -tion/-ation (the act of), -ness (condition of), -ion (state/action), -ing (activity), -ment (state/action), -ity (state/quality), -ism (condition/state of), -dom (area/condition), -ship (condition/state)

Possible Answers
1. person who analyses (analyst)
2. person who compiles (compiler)
3. a machine that calculates (calculator)
4. a machine that processes information (processor)
5. state of being compiled (compilation)
6. condition of being ready (readiness)
7. condition of being clean (cleanliness)
8. condition of being happy (happiness)
9. one who types (typist)
10. one who plays the piano (pianist)
11. pertaining to electricity (electrician)
12. state of performing (performance)
13. quality of being independent (independence)
14. one who programs (programmer)
15. one who operates something (operator)
16. state of conversing (conversion)
17. activity of many tasks (multitasking)
18. act of measuring (measurement)
19. state required (requirement)
20. state of being electrical (electricity)
21. condition of being magnetic (magnetism)
22. free domain (freedom)
23. state of being partners (partnership)
24. one who writes (writer)

Published by Frank Schaffer Publications.
Copyright protected.

0-7682-3413-1
101 Easy Reading Games

Anytime Brain Builders

 **Details—Little Details**

Objective: introduce and reinforce story details

Materials: fables (pages 56, 59, and 63), whiteboard (or overhead, chalkboard, or chart paper), pencils, and paper

Getting Ready:
1. Read the original fables aloud.
2. Divide players into four teams.

Setting: Teams gather at the board.

How to Play: Ask a question. The first player to answer correctly wins a point for her team. As you play, keep score on the board.

Challenges
1. In "The Hungry Wolf and the Lost Lamb," what was the wolf's first accusation? (the lamb had insulted him)
2. In "Two Dogs," what was the house dog trained to do? (watch the house)
3. In "The Lion and the Boar," where did the animals meet? (at a well)
4. In "The Donkey's Shadow," why did the man who owned the donkey go with the traveler? (to bring home his donkey)
5. In "The Father and Two Daughters," what was the first daughter's occupation? (gardener)
6. In the beginning of "Three Travelers," describe where they climbed. (the top of a tall cliff overlooking the sea)
7. In "The Battle," who suggested using bricks? (the bricklayer)
8. In "The Hungry Wolf and the Lost Lamb," why did the lamb say he had never eaten grass? (he still drank his mother's milk)
9. In "Two Dogs," what was the second dog trained to do? (hunt)
10. In "The Lion and the Boar," what did the animals fight over? (who would drink first)
11. In "The Donkey's Shadow," where did the traveler want to sit? (under the donkey)
12. In "The Father and Two Daughters," what did the tile maker wish? (for dry weather)
13. In the end of "Three Travelers," what was the second thing they thought they saw? (a small boat)
14. In "The Battle," who suggested using animal skins for protection? (the hunter)
15. In the "Hungry Wolf and the Lost Lamb," how many accusations did the wolf make? (three)
16. In "Two Dogs," what did the master give the house dog? (meat)
17. In "The Lion and the Boar," what was the third animal mentioned? (vultures)
18. In "The Donkey's Shadow," how did the donkey owner get home? (he walked)

Published by Frank Schaffer Publications.
Copyright protected.

0-7682-3413-1
101 Easy Reading Games

Anytime Brain Builders

78 Which Came First?

Objective: introduce and reinforce sequence of events

Materials: list of word pairs (see below)

Setting: Players gather at the board.

How to Play: Name two things. Players tell which comes first and last.

Alternate Version: Repeat word list. Players tell which comes first in ABC order, favorite and least favorite, etc.

Word Pairs List
September/October
Christmas/Fourth of July
hundreds/thousands
morning/evening
sunrise/sunset
dawn/dusk
autumn/spring
Civil War/World War II
George Washington/Abraham Lincoln
Tuesday/Friday

79 First or Last?

Objective: introduce and reinforce sequence of events and details

Materials: fables (pages 56, 59, and 63), whiteboard (or overhead, chalkboard, or chart paper), pencils, and paper

Setting: Students gather at the board.

How to Play: Read aloud the fables. Ask questions, similar to the sample questions (below), regarding sequencing of events.

Sample Questions
1. In "The Donkey's Shadow," which came first? (quarrel/donkey galloped off)
2. In "The Lion and the Boar," which came first? (vultures flew over/animals were thirsty)
3. In "The Two Dogs," which came first? (hunting dog complained/house dog explained)
4. In "The Hungry Wolf and the Lost Lamb," which came last? (wolf resolved not to eat the lamb/wolf ate the lamb)
5. In "The Father and Two Daughters," who spoke first? (daughter who wanted rain/daughter who didn't want rain)
6. In "Three Travelers," did the travelers think they saw the boat or ship first? (ship/boat)
7. In "The Battle," the first speaker was whom? (bricklayer/carpenter/hunter)

Anytime Brain Builders

80 | Who Might Have Said It?

Objective: reinforce comprehension of dialogue and author purpose

Materials: fables (pages 56, 59, and 63), whiteboard (or overhead, chalkboard, or chart paper), pencils, and paper

Getting Ready: Read the seven original fables aloud. List the numbered titles on the board.
1. "The Hungry Wolf and Lost Lamb"
2. "Two Dogs"
3. "The Lion and the Boar"
4. "The Donkey's Shadow"
5. "The Father and Two Daughters"
6. "Three Travelers"
7. "The Battle"

Setting: Students gather at the board.

How to Play: Read a line, and players indicate the fable from which the line might have come with a show of fingers. Then ask a player to name the character who might have said it. (Answers may vary.)

List of Lines
1. "Who said that you could come into my pasture to graze?" (1—the wolf)
2. "I am hot and need some shade, too." (7—donkey's owner)
3. "If we keep fighting like this, we might end up dead." (3—lion or boar, or 7—one of the men)
4. "I wish we hadn't wasted our time." (6—one of the three travelers)
5. "I wish it would rain." (5—gardener)
6. "I hope the ship has treasures." (6—one of the three travelers)
7. "Brick is the best!" (7—bricklayer)
8. "Nooooooooo, please don't eat me." (1—lamb)
9. "I hope it doesn't rain." (5—tile maker)
10. "You think I like being cooped up all day?" (2—house dog)
11. "This donkey belongs to me." (4—owner)
12. "Those vultures are waiting for us to kill each other." (3—lion or boar)
13. "Father, come look at my roses." (5—gardener)
14. "You don't deserve this meat." (2—hunting dog)
15. "I should get to drink here first; I am king of the jungle." (3—lion)
16. "Wood is the strongest defense." (7—carpenter)
17. "Leather is stronger than bricks or wood." (7—hunter)
18. "A tyrant always makes excuses for his tyraaaaaany." (1—lamb)
19. "Am I responsible for my poor training?" (2—house dog)
20. "I am so hot and thirsty." (3—lion or boar, 6—one of the three travelers, or 4—traveler or owner of donkey)

Published by Frank Schaffer Publications.
Copyright protected.

0-7682-3413-1
101 Easy Reading Games

Anytime Brain Builders

 Lessons Learned

Objective: introduce and reinforce predicting author's intent

Materials: fables (pages 56, 59, and 63), whiteboard (or overhead, chalkboard, or chart paper)

Getting Ready:
1. Read the seven original fables aloud.
2. List the fables on the board.

Setting: Pair students and gather at the board.

How to Play:
1. Name a lesson (offered by Aesop; see list below).
2. Players guess which fable Aesop had in mind.

Aesop's Lessons
1. The tyrant will always find an excuse for his tyranny. ("The Hungry Wolf and the Lost Lamb")
2. Children are not to be blamed for the faults of their parents. ("The Two Dogs")
3. It is better to make friends than to become the food of vultures. ("The Lion and the Boar")
4. In quarreling about the shadow, we often lose the substance. ("The Donkey's Shadow")
5. One cannot always please his children. ("The Father and Two Daughters")
6. Our mere anticipations of life outrun its realities. ("Three Travelers")
7. Every man for himself. ("The Battle")

Alternate Version: Make a list of other possible lessons learned in fables.

 Before or After?

Objective: introduce and reinforce sequence of events and details.

Materials: fables (pages 56, 59, and 63), whiteboard (or overhead, chalkboard, or chart paper)

Setting: Students gather at the board.

How to Play:
1. Read aloud two sentences from the same fable.
2. Players say which came first.
3. As you play, keep score on the board.

Anytime Brain Builders

 **Lessons Learned in Fairy Tales**

Objective: predict author's intent

Materials: fairy tale lessons (see list below)

Setting: Players gather at the board.

How to Play: Name each lesson; players name an appropriate fairy tale.

Fairy Tale Lessons

1. Beware of the wolf. (answer will vary)
2. Don't go into the woods. (Hansel and Gretel, Little Red Riding Hood)
3. Don't enter without knocking. (The Three Bears)
4. Beauty is in the eye of the beholder. (The Ugly Duckling, Beauty and the Beast)
5. If you lie sometimes, people won't ever trust you. (The Boy Who Cried Wolf)
6. A thing worth doing is worth doing well. (The Three Little Pigs)
7. You can't fool everyone—especially a child. (The Emperor's New Clothes)
8. Slow and easy wins the race. (The Tortoise and the Hare)
9. If someone is lying, it's as clear as the nose on his face. (Pinocchio)
10. Be kind, even to those who mistreat you. (Cinderella)
11. Clothes don't make the man. (The Emperor's New Clothes)
12. Never go into the woods without a map. (Hansel and Gretel)

 **Rebus Compounds**

Objective: introduce and reinforce twenty-one compound words

Materials: Compound Word cards (page 123), wipe-off board

Getting Ready:
1. Reproduce cards for each pair of students.
2. Explain that all of the answers will be a compound word.
3. Have students pick a partner. Give each pair a set of cards.

Setting: Pairs work at desks or a table with a working surface.

How to Play:
1. Players have seven minutes to make up and draw rebus riddles as their partners try to decode as many compound words as they can.
2. The pair with the most decoded words is declared the winner.

Anytime Brain Builders

 **Homophone Riddles**

Objective: introduce and reinforce homophone pairs

Materials: whiteboard (or overhead, chalkboard, or chart paper) stopwatch, list of homophone clues (see below)

Getting Ready:
1. Review the term *homophone* (words that sound the same but have different meanings and spellings).
2. Divide students into four teams.

Setting: Teams gather at the board.

How to Play:
1. A member of each team stands at the board.
2. Give a homophone clue and start the timer for one minute.
3. Players are to write both homophones.
4. Each correct answer wins a point for that player's team.
5. As you play, keep score on the board and make a list of homophone pairs on the board.

Homophone Clues
1. an insect and your mother's sister (ant, aunt)
2. an animal and to be naked (bear, bare)
4. to exist and buzzing animal (be, bee)
5. doe or buck and beloved (deer, dear)
6. female deer and uncooked bread (doe, dough)
7. female sheep and yourself (ewe, you)
8. two female sheep and to apply (ewes, use)
9. African antelope and not old (gnu, new)
10. several antelopes and timely information (gnus, news)
11. a rabbit and it grows from your head (hare, hair)
12. cowboy's friend and rough voice (horse, hoarse)
13. a mollusk and fibrous contracting tissue (mussel, muscle)
14. a large oceanic mammal and a cry (whale, wail)
15. a long-haired ox and informal talk (yak, yack)

Published by Frank Schaffer Publications.
Copyright protected.

0-7682-3413-1
101 Easy Reading Games

Anytime Brain Builders

86   Make a Word

Objective: introduce and reinforce adding prefixes and suffixes to twenty root words

Materials: Root Word cards (page 116), sturdy cardstock, scissors, rubber band

Getting Ready:
1. Reproduce cards.
2. Cut apart cards and secure with a rubber band.
3. Make a list of prefixes and suffixes on the board (see lists below).
4. Divide students into four teams.

Setting: Teams gather at the board.

How to Play:
1. Shuffle the deck of cards and place facedown.
2. A player from each team stands at the board.
3. Turn over and read the top Root Word card.
4. The first player to write a word using the root plus a prefix or/and suffix wins a point (or two) for his team. A word with a prefix or a suffix is one point. A word with a prefix and a suffix is two points.
5. As you play, keep score on the board and make a word list.

Prefixes List

un-, non-, in-, dis-, re-, semi-, mini-, micro-, inter-, super-, trans-, ex-, extra-, peri-, pre-, ante-, fore-, post-

Suffixes List

-ance, -ence, -or, -er, -ist, -ize, -ate, -fly, -en, -ify, -able, -ible, -less, -ic, -icle, -ish, -ive, -ly

Possible Answers

unhappily, nonexistence, disappearance, reestablished, semidarkness, minicomputer, microscopic, interspacing, transportable, exchangeable, extraordinarily, prescribing, anticlimactic, forerunner, postmarked, unacceptable

Anytime Brain Builders

87 The Big Unscramble

Objective: introduce and reinforce words that have both a prefix and a suffix (see list below)

Materials: The Big Unscramble Game Sheet (page 89), pencils, stopwatch

Getting Ready:
1. Reproduce The Big Unscramble game sheet for each pair of students.
2. Explain that all of the answers will be words containing a prefix and a suffix.
3. Pair the students.
4. Give each pair a game sheet.

Setting: Pairs work at desks or a table with a working surface.

How to Play:
1. Players have 20 minutes to unscramble as many words as they can.
2. The pair with the most unscrambled words wins.

Word List

unhappily, nonexistence, disappearance, reestablished, semidarkness, minicomputer, microscopic, interspacing, transportable, exchangeable, extraordinarily, prescribing, anticlimactic, forerunner, postmarked, unacceptable

88 Scrambled Words

Objective: unscramble other categories of words

How to Play: Use the same rules as The Big Unscramble. One at a time, write the scrambled words on the board.

Categories
- rhyming words scramble; use -ize/-ise cards, -ache/-ake/-eak cards, and -ee/-y cards (pages 98–100)
- prefix words scramble; use Prefix word cards (pages 111–112)
- noun and verb scramble; use Noun and Verb word cards (pages 113–114)
- homophone, synonym, antonym scramble; use Homophone, Synonym, Antonym word cards (pages 117–120)

The Big Unscramble Game Sheet

1. root means glad

   upilynpha _____

2. root means to live

   nstceoennexi _____

3. root means to be seen

   dpncepearaisa _____

4. root means to create

   hedrstabliees _____

5. root means not light

   neessmidark _____

6. root means to figure

   inicuterompm _____

7. root means to see

   roicpicscom _____

8. root means a place

   inpersgacint _____

9. root means take it

   acctaeunblep _____

10. root is a spot/place

    tnsableportra _____

11. root means reverse

    eanablegexch _____

12. root means common

    etraarilyordinx _____

13. root means to write

    pregscribin _____

14. root means ending

    licaamticntic _____

15. root means move forward

    orunreenrf _____

16. root means to indicate

    ostmedarpk _____

Total Points: _____

Anytime Brain Builders

89   I Spy a Noun/Verb

Objective: introduce and reinforce nouns and verbs (see list below)

Materials: word list, whiteboard (or overhead, chalkboard, or chart paper)

Getting Ready: On the board, print the nouns and verbs.

Setting: Players gather at the board.

How to Play: Give word clues as players take turns guessing. Explain that a word may be used more than one time in the game.

Word Clues

1. I spy a noun who rides a one-wheeled vehicle. (unicyclist)
2. I spy a noun who makes quilts. (quilter)
3. I spy a verb that rhymes with mile. (smile)
4. I spy two actions that end with an "f" sound. (cough, laugh)
5. I spy a verb that means fast. (zoom)
6. I spy two nouns that rhyme with fan. (man, woman)
7. I spy four actions that rhyme with eight. (congratulate, illustrate, negotiate, operate)
8. I spy a word that can be a noun or an action and rhymes with spout. (knockout)
9. I spy an action that rhymes with stint. (fingerprint)
10. I spy a verb that is a slow walk. (plod)
11. I spy a verb that means to think about the past. (remember)
12. I spy a noun who fixes things. (repairman)
13. I spy a verb needed to enjoy food. (taste)
14. I spy a verb that involves tossing things in the air. (juggle)
15. I spy a noun who brings food to others. (waitress)
16. I spy a noun who makes music. (violinist)
17. I spy a verb that means to draw and the person who does it. (illustrate/illustrator)
18. I spy a noun who spends time on the water. (sailor)
19. I spy a noun who lives next door. (neighbor)
20. I spy nouns who rhyme with door. (aviator, doctor, inspector, janitor, neighbor, operator)

Nouns and Verbs List

applaud, aviator, boast, captain, congratulate, cough, display, doctor, entwine, farmer, fingerprint, glance, golfer, heave, housekeeper, illustrate, inspector, illustrator, janitor, juggle, king, knockout, label, lawyer, laugh, man, memorize, negotiate, neighbor, operate, operator, plod, policeman, queen, quilter, remember, repairman, sailor, smile, senior, taste, unicyclist, unfold, vaporize, violinist, waitress, woman, zoom

90   I Spy a Homophone

Use the same rules as I Spy a Noun/Verb to introduce and reinforce homophone pairs. See page 86 for a list of homophone pairs to be listed on the board. Use the homophone riddles as clues.

Published by Frank Schaffer Publications.
Copyright protected.

0-7682-3413-1
101 Easy Reading Games

Kinesthetic / Moving Games

91 Writing Relay

Objective: introduce and reinforce using punctuation marks

Materials: What If? cards (page 125), whiteboard (or overhead, chalkboard, or chart paper)

Getting Ready: Divide students into four teams.

Setting: Teams gather at the board.

How to Play:
1. A member of each team stands at the board.
2. Dictate a What If? sentence.
3. The first player writes as much of the sentence as he remembers. Then he tags a member of his team.
4. The second person adds to the sentence, words, punctuation, and so on, and tags the third member of the team.
5. Repeat the sentence often.
6. The first team to write the whole sentence correctly, including spelling and punctuation, wins a point.
7. Repeat with the next sentence.
8. At the end of thirteen rounds, declare the winners!

92 Learning Key

Objective: introduce and reinforce words that rhyme with key (see list below)

Materials: -ee/-y cards (page 100), paper cutter, rubber bands

Getting Ready:
1. Reproduce a set of word cards for each student.
2. Cut apart cards and secure each deck with a rubber band.

Setting: Pairs sit on the floor or outside in the grass.

How to Play: Shuffle cards and take turns lining cards up alphabetically in train fashion. The first person who places cards in the line in ABC order is the winner.

Word List
bumblebee, honeybee, chimpanzee, chickadee, Tennessee, bakery, celebrity, dignity, ebony, fiery, gravity, Italy, liberty, mystery, necessity, poetry, privacy, rivalry, salary, silvery, sugary, unity, vanity, wintry

Kinesthetic / Moving Games

 **Action!**

Objective: introduce and reinforce verbs

Materials: Verb cards (page 113), scissors, paper bag

Getting Ready:
1. Reproduce the word cards.
2. Cut apart cards and fold each one.
3. Place in a paper bag.

Setting: Students gather at the board.

How to Play:
1. Players take turns drawing a verb from the bag and doing a charade or giving verbal hints. **Example:** boast—I did a great thing today!
2. Others shout out their guesses. When a player guesses correctly, he must spell the word to get a point.
3. As you play, keep score on the board and make a word list.

Alternate Version: Play the same way with Noun cards (page 114).

 **Compound Charades**

Objective: introduce and reinforce twenty-one compound words

Materials: Compound Word cards (page 123), paper bag, whiteboard (or overhead, chalkboard, or chart paper)

Getting Ready:
1. Copy and cut apart the word cards.
2. Put the word cards in a paper bag.
3. Explain that all of the answers will be a compound word.
4. Divide students into four teams.

Setting: Teams gather at the board.

How to Play:
1. The first player draws a card and charades the two word parts to make the word.
2. The first player to guess the compound word wins a point for her team.
3. As you play, keep score on the board and make a word list.

95 Double Trouble

Objective: introduce and reinforce verbs and nouns

Materials: Verb cards (page 113), Noun cards (page 114), scissors, two paper bags, whiteboard (or overhead, chalkboard, or chart paper)

Getting Ready:
1. Reproduce the word cards.
2. Cut apart cards and fold each one.
3. Place the Verb cards in one paper bag and the Noun cards in the other.
4. Divide students into four teams.

Setting: Teams gather at the board.

How to Play:
1. Players take turns drawing a word from each bag.
2. Without saying the words, a player must convey the noun and verb through dialogue. **Example:** "Come into my castle, and I will introduce you to the queen." (welcome/king)
3. All players may shout out their answer.
4. The first player to correctly name the noun and verb wins a point for his team and gets to be It next.
5. The first team to get 6 points is declared the winner.
6. As you play, keep score on the board and make a list of the noun/verb combinations.

Alternate Version: Use the list of noun/verb combinations to write skits, jokes, or short stories.

96 "What If" Skits

Objective: introduce and reinforce making predictions

Materials: fables (pages 56, 59, and 63), What If? cards (page 125)

Getting Ready:
1. List the fables on the board.
2. Divide students into teams of three or four.

Setting: Teams gather at the board.

How to Play:
1. Each group draws a card from the bag.
2. Give players time to discuss the possibilities and vote on their favorite.
3. Then they are to make up a skit, and through dialogue, demonstrate the ideas.
4. Allow plenty of time for rehearsal.
5. In a large group, take turns performing skits while the others try to guess the fable and the "what if."

Kinesthetic / Moving Games

 **Fact or Opinion?**

Objective: introduce and reinforce distinguishing facts and opinions

Materials: fables (pages 56, 59, and 63), whiteboard (or overhead, chalkboard, or chart paper)

Getting Ready:
1. Read the seven original fables aloud.
2. Teach students sign language for letters "f" and "o."

Setting: Students gather at the board.

How to Play: As you make statements, players use sign language to indicate fact or opinion.

Fact or Opinion Statements
1. In "The Hungry Wolf and the Lost Lamb," the wolf was very bad. (O)
2. In "Two Dogs," the hunting dog was greedy. (O)
3. In "The Lion and the Boar," the lion and boar were thirsty. (F)
4. In "The Donkey's Shadow," the owner didn't like the man who rented his donkey. (O)
5. In "The Father and Two Daughters," one daughter wished for rain. (F)
6. In the beginning of "Three Travelers," they had high hopes. (F)
7. In "The Battle," The bricklayer was right. (O)

8. In "The Hungry Wolf and the Lost Lamb," the lamb was afraid. (F)
9. In "Two Dogs," the house dog was lazy. (O)
10. In "The Lion and the Boar," the animals finally agreed. (F)
11. In "The Donkey's Shadow," the donkey went home. (F)
12. In "The Father and Two Daughters," the tile maker wished for dry weather. (F)
13. In the end of "Three Travelers," their hopes were dashed. (F)
14. In "The Battle," the carpenter had a strong opinion. (F)
15. The "Hungry Wolf and the Lost Lamb," the lamb was sensible. (F)
16. In "Two Dogs," the master was foolish. (O)
17. In "The Lion and the Boar," the vultures were evil. (O)
18. In "The Donkey's Shadow," the donkey's owner had to walk home. (F)
19. In "The Father and His Two Daughters," the father didn't know what to wish for. (F)
20. In "Three Travelers," they went home disappointed. (F)
21. In "The Battle," the battle would have been won if the men could have agreed. (O)

Published by Frank Schaffer Publications.

0-7682-3413-1
101 Easy Reading Games

Kinesthetic / Moving Games

 **Run and Read Animals**

Objective: introduce and reinforce animal words

Materials: Animal Word cards (pages 101–104), sturdy cardstock, paper cutter, rubber bands

Getting Ready:
1. Reproduce cards four times.
2. Cut apart cards and secure each deck with a rubber band.
3. Divide students into four teams.

Setting: Outdoors; each team lines up on cement or asphalt.

How to Play:
1. Place stacks of cards 10 feet apart.
2. Group team lines about 20 feet from cards.
3. Call out the name of an animal.
4. The first player on each team runs to that team's cards and flips through it to find the word, then brings it back to the teacher. The first player back wins a point for his team.
5. Repeat with another animal, and the second member of each team races to find it.

 **Other Run and Read Games**

Use the same game rules to reinforce many words. Use any of the following card combinations.
- rhyming words (pages 98–100)
- prefix/suffix words (pages 111–112)
- nouns and verbs (pages 113–114)
- homophone, synonym, antonyms (pages 117–120)

Published by Frank Schaffer Publications.
Copyright protected.

0-7682-3413-1
101 Easy Reading Games

Kinesthetic / Moving Games

 **Body Language—Homophones**

Objective: introduce and reinforce pairs of homophones

Materials: Homophone cards (pages 121–122), scissors, paper bag

Getting Ready:
1. Reproduce the word cards.
2. Cut apart cards and fold each one.
3. Place the cards in a paper bag.

Setting: Students gather at the board.

How to Play:
1. Players take turns drawing a word from the bag.
2. They are to use their bodies (fingers, arms, legs, etc.) to indicate the letters of the word.
3. Players take turns spelling their guesses.
4. The first player to correctly spell the word gets to draw the next card from the bag.

 **Other Body Language Games**

Use the same game rules to introduce and reinforce spelling of other words with any of these word cards:

- rhyming word cards; use -ize/-ise cards, -ache/-ake/-eak cards, and -ee/-y cards (pages 98–100)
- prefix/suffix words (pages 111–112)
- nouns and verbs (pages 113–114)
- homophones, synonyms, antonyms (pages 117–120)
- animal word cards (101–104)

Clueless Cards

Use with Activities: 58

A drink not good with *marmalade*—3 syllables (lemonade)	A way to walk for a *gag*—2 syllables (zigzag)
A book to put in your *backpack*—3 syllables (paperback)	Animal never found on a *wedding cake*—3 syllables (rattlesnake)
Place the baseballs sometimes *land*—2 syllables (grandstand)	Some people think this place is a *wonderland*—3 syllables (Disneyland)
Wouldn't want it to land in your *meringue*—3 syllables (boomerang)	It is another way to *evaluate*—3 syllables (estimate)
This pet isn't *very big*—3 syllables, 2 words (guinea pig)	Skiing this can be quite a *thrill*—2 syllables (downhill)
This shoe might be made of *lambskin*—3 syllables (moccasin)	It is a quiet way of *visiting*—3 syllables (whispering)
This pest is seldom seen in *sunlight*—2 syllables (termite)	This kind of person is seldom *cooperative*—3 syllables (negative)
It's not walking on the *sidewalk*—2 syllables (jaywalk)	This hole in a board is bigger than a *pinhole*—2 syllables (knothole)
Some think it is an *ice storm*—2 syllables (hailstorm)	It's a photo of someone with a *slingshot*—2 syllables (snapshot)
At the fights, some *look out* for this—2 syllables (knockout)	This duck-billed creature is not an *octopus*—3 syllables (platypus)

-ize/-ise cards

Use with Activities: 1, 11, 13, 23, 46, 53, 59, 68, 88, 99, 101

advise	agonize	analyze	apologize
arise	authorize	capsize	categorize
clockwise	comprise	criticize	demise
despise	devise	disguise	emphasize
exercise	harmonize	likewise	materialize
surprise	realize	revise	unwise

Published by Frank Schaffer Publications.
Copyright protected.

0-7682-3413-1
101 Easy Reading Games

-ache/-ake/-eak cards

Use with Activities: 1, 13, 23, 46, 53, 59, 66, 68, 88, 99, 101

awake	backache	beefcake	bellyache
coffeecake	cornflake	cupcake	daybreak
earthquake	forsake	fruitcake	handshake
heartache	johnnycake	mistake	namesake
opaque	outbreak	pancake	rattlesnake
shortcake	snowflake	sweepstake	undertake

Published by Frank Schaffer Publications.
Copyright protected.

0-7682-3413-1
101 Easy Reading Games

-ee/-y cards

Use with Activities: 1, 13, 23, 46, 53, 59, 68, 88, 92, 99, 101

bumblebee	honeybee	chimpanzee	chickadee
Tennessee	bakery	celebrity	dignity
ebony	fiery	gravity	Italy
liberty	mystery	necessity	poetry
privacy	rivalry	salary	silvery
sugary	unity	vanity	wintry

0-7682-3413-1
101 Easy Reading Games

Animal Word Cards

Use with Activities: 2, 10, 14, 25, 40, 42, 49, 52, 62, 69, 75, 98, 101

alligator	alpaca	anaconda	armadillo
badger	beagle	bighorn	blackbird
bobcat	buffalo	bulldog	bullfrog
butterfly	bumblebee	centipede	cheetah
chimpanzee	cobra	coyote	crab

0-7682-3413-1
101 Easy Reading Games

Animal Word Cards (cont.)

dinosaur	dodo	dolphin	donkey
dragonfly	eagle	electric eel	elephant
flamingo	gecko	gazelle	giraffe
gorilla	grasshopper	hamster	hedgehog
hippopotamus	hummingbird	hyena	iguana

0-7682-3413-1
101 Easy Reading Games

Animal Word Cards (cont.)

jellyfish	kangaroo	kiwi	koala
ladybug	lizard	leopard	lobster
manatee	monkey	muskrat	mosquito
octopus	ostrich	panda	peacock
pelican	penguin	prairie dog	platypus

Published by Frank Schaffer Publications.
0-7682-3413-1
101 Easy Reading Games

Animal Word Cards (cont.)

puffin	praying mantis	quail	rattlesnake
rhinoceros	roadrunner	salamander	scorpion
sea horse	squirrel	starfish	stingray
swine	unicorn	wallaby	walrus
whale	woodpecker	weasel	zebra

0-7682-3413-1
101 Easy Reading Games

Animal Picture Cards

Use with Activities: 2, 14

Published by Frank Schaffer Publications.
Copyright protected.

0-7682-3413-1
101 Easy Reading Games

Animal Picture Cards (cont.)

Animal Picture Cards (cont.)

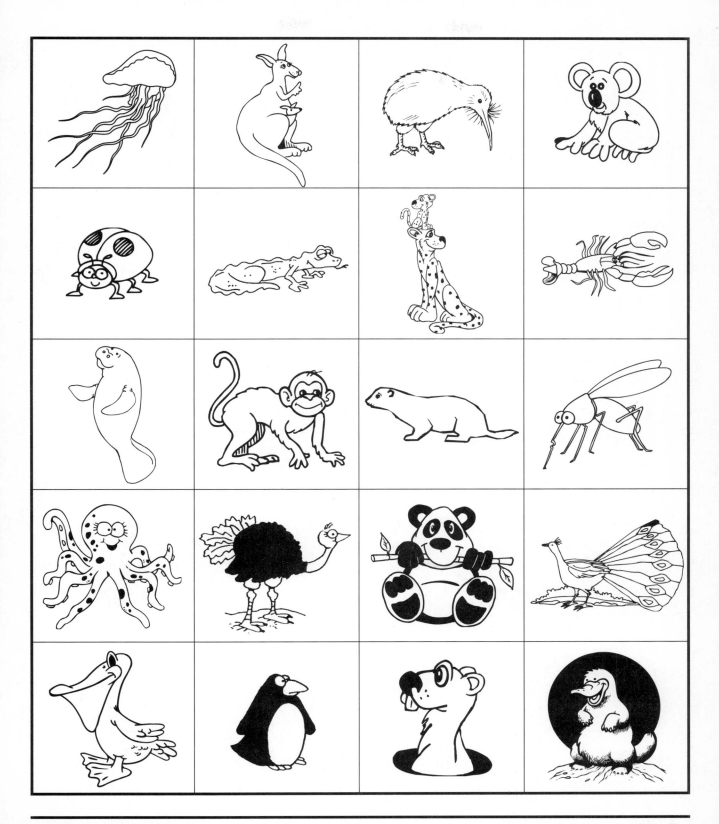

Animal Picture Cards (cont.)

Published by Frank Schaffer Publications.
Copyright protected.

0-7682-3413-1
101 Easy Reading Games

Food Cards

Use with Activities: 2, 15, 37, 43, 54

bologna	banana	bread	blueberries
cabbage	cake	candy	cheese
cherry	croissant	drumstick	lettuce
broccoli	cauliflower	green bean	french fry
grape	hamburger	ice cream	lima bean

Published by Frank Schaffer Publications.

0-7682-3413-1
101 Easy Reading Games

Food Cards (cont.)

muffin	mushroom	macaroni	snow pea
peanut	pepper	pie	pineapple
pizza	popcorn	potato	pumpkin
sandwich	shrimp	soda	beef
strawberry	hot chocolate	tomato	zucchini

Published by Frank Schaffer Publications.

0-7682-3413-1
101 Easy Reading Games

Prefix Word Cards

Use with Activities: 17, 44, 48, 88, 99, 101

interdependent	interactive	interpose	interplay
superpower	supersaturate	supermarket	superman
transmit	transform	transient	transmarine
exit	exclude	excise	excerpt
extraordinary	extreme	extrovert	extrasensory
submerge	submarine	subordinate	subside
infraction	infrared	infringe	infuse
periodic	peripheral	periscope	periscopic

Published by Frank Schaffer Publications.

0-7682-3413-1
101 Easy Reading Games

Numeric Prefix Word cards

Use with Activities: 39, 44, 48, 88, 99, 101

semicircle	semifinal	semimonthly	monochromatic
monocular	monocycle	monochord	monologue
binary	bicycle	bicuspid	biaxial
tricycle	triangle	tripod	quadrant
quadrillion	quadruplet	pentagon	pentacle
pentagonal	hexagon	hexagram	hexameter
septet	octopus	octagon	decimal
decigram	decimeter	multiplication	multimillionaire

0-7682-3413-1
101 Easy Reading Games

Verb Cards

Use with Activities: 3, 16, 38, 61, 88, 93, 95, 99, 101

applaud	boast	congratulate	display
entwine	fingerprint	glance	heave
illustrate	juggle	knockout	label
memorize	negotiate	operate	plod
quilt	remember	snooze	taste
unfold	vaporize	welcome	zoom

Noun Cards

Use with Activities: 3, 16, 38, 61, 88, 93, 95, 99, 101

aviator	beauty queen	captain	doctor
elevator operator	farmer	golfer	housekeeper
inspector	janitor	king	lawyer
mechanic	neighbor	operator	policeman
queen	repairman	senior	trapeze artist
unicyclist	violinist	waitress	x-ray technician

Published by Frank Schaffer Publications.
Copyright protected.

0-7682-3413-1
101 Easy Reading Games

Noun-Forming Suffixes Cards

Use with Activity: 76

performance	independence	programmer	operator
writer	compiler	calculator	processor
analyst	typist	pianist	electrician
compilation	readiness	cleanliness	happiness
conversion	multitasking	measurement	requirement
electricity	magnetism	freedom	partnership

Root Word Cards

Use with Activities: 45, 86

happy	exist	secure	appear
establish	dark	compute	space
enjoy	partner	port	change
ordinary	scope	climax	scribe
run	mark	human	accept

Homophone, Synonym, Antonym Cards

Use with Activities: 19, 31, 51, 60, 88, 99, 101

Word: add	**Word:** ate	**Word:** bare	**Word:** bury	**Word:** beat
H: ad	**H:** eight	**H:** bear	**H:** berry	**H:** beet
S: increase	**S:** consumed	**S:** nude	**S:** entomb	**S:** weary
A: subtract	**A:** starved	**A:** dressed	**A:** uncover	**A:** energetic
Word: boy	**Word:** ceiling	**Word:** chilly	**Word:** close	**Word:** coarse
H: buoy	**H:** sealing	**H:** chili	**H:** clothes	**H:** course
S: lad	**S:** roof	**S:** cool	**S:** shut	**S:** rough
A: girl	**A:** floor	**A:** warm	**A:** open	**A:** smooth
Word: freeze	**Word:** new	**Word:** higher	**Word:** him	**Word:** whole
H: frees	**H:** gnu	**H:** hire	**H:** hymn	**H:** hole
S: chill	**S:** unused	**S:** elevated	**S:** he	**S:** all
A: boil	**A:** old	**A:** lower	**A:** her	**A:** part
Word: flee	**Word:** male	**Word:** merry	**Word:** minor	**Word:** none
H: flea	**H:** mail	**H:** marry	**H:** miner	**H:** nun
S: run	**S:** man	**S:** happy	**S:** unimportant	**S:** zero
A: stay	**A:** female	**A:** sad	**A:** major	**A:** some
Word: pale	**Word:** past	**Word:** patience	**Word:** real	**Word:** wee
H: pail	**H:** passed	**H:** patients	**H:** reel	**H:** we
S: light	**S:** before	**S:** endurance	**S:** authentic	**S:** small
A: bright	**A:** future	**A:** impatience	**A:** fake	**A:** large

0-7682-3413-1
101 Easy Reading Games

Homophone, Synonym, Antonym Cards (cont.)

Use with Activities: 19, 51, 88, 99, 101

ceiling	sealing	roof	floor
chilly	chili	cool	warm
close	clothes	shut	open
coarse	course	rough	smooth
die	dye	dead	born
freeze	frees	chill	boil

0-7682-3413-1
101 Easy Reading Games

Homophone, Synonym, Antonym Cards (cont.)

Use with Activities: 19, 51, 88, 99, 101

new	gnu	unused	old
higher	hire	elevated	lower
him	hymn	he	her
whole	hole	all	part
flee	flea	run	stay
male	mail	man	female

Homophone, Synonym, Antonym Cards (cont.)

Use with Activities: 19, 51, 88, 99, 101

merry	marry	happy	sad
minor	miner	trivial	major
none	nun	zero	some
pale	pail	light	bright
past	passed	before	future
patience	patients	forbearance	impatience

0-7682-3413-1
101 Easy Reading Games

Homophone Cards

Use with Activities: 4, 18, 26, 50, 100

ant	aunt	bear	bare
piece	peace	doe	dough
ewe	you	ewes	use

0-7682-3413-1
101 Easy Reading Games

Homophone Cards

Use with Activities: 18, 26, 50, 100

gnus

news

hare

hair

flour

flower

son

sun

yak

yack

gnu

new

Published by Frank Schaffer Publications.
Copyright protected.

0-7682-3413-1
101 Easy Reading Games

Compound Word Cards

Use with Activities: 84, 94

anyone	basketball	blacktop
bluebird	bulldog	butterfly
chairman	cheesecake	cowboy
cupboard	doorbell	football
gingerbread	keyboard	ladybug
mailbox	horsefly	starfish
seesaw	skateboard	someone

Published by Frank Schaffer Publications.
0-7682-3413-1
101 Easy Reading Games

Fairy Tale Cards

Use with Activities: 36, 47

The Three Little Pigs	Goldilocks and the Three Bears	Cinderella	The Three Billy Goats Gruff
Peter Rabbit	Sleeping Beauty	Snow White and the Seven Dwarfs	Hansel and Gretel
The Ugly Duckling	The Emperor's New Clothes	Pinocchio	Rumpelstiltskin
Chicken Little	The Little Red Hen	Little Red Riding Hood	The Boy Who Cried Wolf
The Tortoise and the Hare	The Little Mermaid	Beauty and the Beast	The Princess and the Pea
Jack and the Beanstalk	The Gingerbread Man	Rapunzel	The Frog Prince

Published by Frank Schaffer Publications.

0-7682-3413-1
101 Easy Reading Games

What If Cards

Use with Activities: 8, 91, 96

What if in the fable, "The Father and Two Daughters," the father had been a farmer?	What if in the fable, "Three Travelers," there had been a ship—a pirate's ship—and the travelers had been captured?
What if in the fable, "The Battle," all three men had been blacksmiths?	What if in the fable, "Two Dogs," the dogs had gotten into a fight?
What if in the fable, "The Lion and the Boar," the well had been dry?	What if in the fable, "The Donkey's Shadow," it had been winter?
What if in the fable, "The Hungry Wolf and Lost Lamb," the shepherd had come looking for the lamb?	What if in the fable, "The Father and Two Daughters," the daughters had both been ballerinas?
What if in the "Three Travelers," the travelers had been in too much of a hurry to stop to watch a ship?	What if in the fable, "The Battle," the men had been a butcher, a baker, and a candlestick maker?
What if in the fable, "The Two Dogs," the hunting dog had died?	What if in the fable, "The Lion and the Boar," the lion had fell into the well?
What if in the fable, "The Donkey's Shadow," it had been cloudy and there was no sun to make shadows?	(make up your own)

Situation Cards

Use with Activity: 41

The floor of Lucia's tree house cracked down the middle.	There was an earthquake while the children were at school.
During a scary movie, there was a blackout in the theater.	Flood waters filled Morgan's house.
Elizabeth's grandfather died.	Parker's uncle won a million dollars in a lottery.
Steve's bike was stolen.	Sarah found out that her mother and father were getting a divorce.
Amy's best friend moved away.	Arnie's brother went away to college.
James' father remarried a mean woman.	Jolyn lost her mother's best sweater.
Sam's dog was hit by a car.	Su Lin accidentally started a fire in the kitchen.
Samir was in a car accident.	Paul found out his older brother was a thief.
Emily was playing with a knife and cut herself badly.	Kiesha found pawprints in her garden.

Published by Frank Schaffer Publications.
Copyright protected.

0-7682-3413-1
101 Easy Reading Games

Answer Key

Page 69

1. Max, are you going to the party?
2. We ate pie, ice cream, and cookies.
3. If you don't go, we cannot go.
4. Sue, you misspelled one word.
5. Each one finished (his/her) work.
6. Does that windmill wind in the wind?
7. George will stay, but Regan can't.
8. Juan, you collect snakes, snails, and slugs?
9. Oh dear! I lost the money.
10. It's true—a snail carries its home on its back.

Page 89

The Big Unscramble

1. unhappily
2. nonexistence
3. disappearance
4. reestablished
5. semidarkness
6. minicomputer
7. microscopic
8. interspacing
9. unacceptable
10. transportable
11. exchangeable
12. extraordinarily
13. prescribing
14. anticlimactic
15. forerunner
16. postmarked

Published by Frank Schaffer Publications.
Copyright protected.

0-7682-3413-1
101 Easy Reading Games

Skills Index

(Indexed by game number)

PHONEMIC AWARENESS
- Identify Rhyming Words: 46, 53, 58, 64, 65, 66, 67, 68, 92
- Phonemes: 72
- Syllables: 22, 59

DECODING
- Compound Words: 32, 84, 94
- Contractions: 32
- Plurals: 32, 37, 54
- Prefixes: 17, 27, 39, 44, 45, 48, 73, 86, 87, 88, 99, 101
- Recognizes Common Word Endings
  -ache/-ake/-eak: 1, 13, 23, 46, 53, 66, 68, 88, 99, 101
  -ee/-y: 1, 13, 23, 46, 53, 68, 88, 92, 99, 101
  -ize/-ise: 1, 11, 13, 23, 46, 53, 68, 88, 99, 101
  -oad/-ode: 64
  -out/-oubt/-ought: 65
- Roots: 45, 86
- Suffixes: 45, 73, 76, 86, 87, 99
- Syllables: 22, 59, 75

FLUENCY
- Creative Responses to Text: 57, 95
- Punctuation: 63, 91

VOCABULARY
- Adjectives: 24, 30, 55, 56, 57
- Adverbs: 30
- Antonyms: 19, 31, 32, 51, 60, 88, 99, 101

- Common Sight Words
  -Animals: 2, 10, 14, 25, 40, 42, 49, 52, 62, 67, 69, 75, 98, 101
  -Colors: 20
  -Food: 2, 15, 37, 43, 54
  -Numbers: 21
- Homophones: 4, 18, 19, 26, 31, 33, 50, 51, 60, 85, 88, 90, 99, 100, 101
- Nouns: 3, 16, 24, 30, 38, 55, 56, 57, 61, 88, 89, 93, 95, 99, 101
- Synonyms: 19, 31, 32, 51, 60, 88, 99, 101
- Verbs: 3, 16, 24, 30, 38, 55, 56, 57, 61, 88, 89, 93, 95, 99, 101

COMPREHENSION
- Author's Purpose: 80, 81, 83
- Cause and Effect: 8, 34
- Classifying: 34, 62, 74, 75
- Drawing Conclusions: 34, 41, 83
- Fact or Opinion: 9, 97
- Fantasy and Reality: 6
- Inference: 80
- Main Idea and Details: 77, 79, 82
- Prediction: 34, 81, 96
- Sequencing: 78, 79, 82
- Story Structure: 7, 35, 36, 47

0-7682-3413-1
101 Easy Reading Games